Sport in Brita...

*in the same series*

WEALTH AND INEQUALITY IN BRITAIN
*W. D. Rubenstein*

THE GOVERNMENT OF SPACE
*Alison Ravetz*

EDUCATIONAL OPPORTUNITY AND SOCIAL CHANGE IN ENGLAND
*Michael Sanderson*

A PROPERTY-OWNING DEMOCRACY?
*M. J. Daunton*

THE LABOUR MOVEMENT IN BRITAIN:
A COMMENTARY
*John Saville*

# Sport in Britain

**TONY MASON**

**ff**

*faber and faber*

LONDON · BOSTON

First published in 1988
by Faber and Faber Limited
3 Queen Square London WC1N 3AU

Typeset by Goodfellow & Egan Ltd,
French's Mill, French's Road, Cambridge
Printed in Great Britain by
Richard Clay Ltd, Bungay, Suffolk

*British Library Cataloguing in Publication Data*

Mason, Tony, 1938–
Sport in Britain. — (Historical handbook series).
1. Sports — Social aspects — Great Britain
2. Sports — Economic aspects — Great Britain
I. Title   II. Series
306'.483'0941     GV605

ISBN 0-571-15158-2

# Historical Handbooks

*Series Editors:*
Avner Offer – University of York
F.M.L. Thompson – Institute of Historical Research,
University of London

It is widely recognized that many of the problems of present-day society are deeply rooted in the past, but the actual lines of historical development are often known only to a few specialists, while the policy-makers and analysts themselves frequently rely on a simplified, dramatized, and misleading version of history. Just as the urban landscape of today was largely built in a world that is no longer familiar, so the policy landscape is shaped by attitudes and institutions formed under very different conditions in the past. This series of specially commissioned handbooks aims to provide short, up-to-date studies in the evolution of current problems, not in the form of narratives but as critical accounts of the ways in which the present is formed by the past, and of the roots of present discontents. Designed for those with little time for extensive reading in the specialized literature, the books contain full bibliographies for further study. The authors aim to be as accurate and comprehensive as possible, but not anodyne; their arguments, forcefully expressed, make the historical experience available in challenging form, but do not presume to offer ready-made solutions.

# Contents

Acknowledgements    ix
Preface    xi

1 Introduction: Sport and contemporary society    1
2 Historical development    36
3 Theory and opinion    69
4 Comparisons    94
5 Conclusions    110

Notes    118
Bibliography    121
Index    125

# Acknowledgements

I have talked about sport with many people but so far as this book is concerned I received the most help from David Martin, Jim Obelkevich and Nick Tiratsoo. I should like to thank the Hon. Francis Noel-Baker and the Master, Fellows and Scholars of Churchill College in the University of Cambridge for permission to use the late Lord Noel-Baker's correspondence on page 74. I should also like to thank the BBC and in particular the Written Archives Centre at Caversham Park for allowing me to quote from material located there. Josie Lloyd was an excellent typist and Will Sulkin of Faber and Faber tried his best to improve the manuscript. None of them should be blamed.

# Preface

In 1868 Anthony Trollope listed those sports that were 'essentially dear to the English nature' and were currently having a 'manifest effect on the lives and characters of Englishmen'. He included hunting, shooting, fishing, yachting, rowing, Alpine climbing, racing and cricket, most of which probably would not get into such a list today were one to be compiled by some modern scribe with or without Trollopian and gentlemanly aspirations. Racing, cricket – and perhaps rowing – would, but a 1986 list would also include sports largely ignored in 1868: athletics, boxing, football, rugby (union and league), tennis, badminton, swimming, golf and cycling. Bowls, angling and squash could only be left out at the risk of alienating large proportions of the sporting public and there would be many who would insist on the inclusion of equestrian and motor sports and sailing; not to mention darts and snooker which television coverage has precipitated on to the sports pages. Now sport includes what Trollope might have called games or pastimes. It has become an institutionalized worldwide activity involving millions of people as participants and hundreds of millions as spectators. At a recent count, over thirty sports were to be included in the next Olympics. Although we could not, like Trollope, claim it as a unique part of English or British nature, sport none the less remains an important phenomenon in British society.

The book is divided into five parts. The introductory chapter is devoted to discussion of four of the most important issues relating to British sport in the 1980s: finance, prejudice, drugs and violence. The second chapter surveys historical developments, emphasizing the evolution of distinctions between amateur and professional and the relationship between the growth of sport and that of newspapers, radio and television. It also draws attention to the close connection between sport and gambling. The section entitled 'Theory and Opinion' contains a critical account of neo-Marxist ideas about the role of sport in society, attempts to explain growing levels of participation in a range of sports and notes the criticism of sport's competitive ethos which has accompanied it. Different aspects of the relationship between sport and politics in Britain are dealt with in various parts of the book, but a comparison of the role of the state in the promotion of sport in Britain, Germany, Italy and the Soviet Union forms the focus of the fourth chapter. The concluding discussion explores some of the meanings of sport both for individuals and society.

# 1
## Introduction: Sport and contemporary society

This chapter will examine, in turn, the four most important issues affecting contemporary British sport: money, prejudice, drugs and violence.

Money usually becomes a problem for those who believe they do not have enough of it. In the world of sport in the 1980s that often means everyone except the leading players, their agents, and the promoters most closely associated with them. Most income for sport still comes from people prepared to pay in order to watch. But rising costs of travel, equipment, administration and the salaries of the leading practitioners have meant that the source cannot provide enough

TABLE 1: *Spectating rates: percentage of population watching*

|              | **1973** | **1977** | **1980** |
|--------------|----------|----------|----------|
| Football     | 6.7      | 5.1      | 5.0      |
| Cricket      | 2.5      | 2.0      | 1.5      |
| Horse racing | 0.7      | 1.2      | 1.3      |
| Motor sports | 1.4      | 1.2      | 1.3      |
| Rugby        | 0.7      | 1.2      | 0.9      |
|              | 12.0     | 10.7     | 10.0     |

*Source*: Peter McIntosh and Valerie Charlton, *The Impact of Sport for All Policy 1966–1984 and a Way Forward* (Sports Council 1985) p. 117.

especially in the context of a long-term decline in the numbers of those willing to pay at the gate. This is most marked in Britain's national team games of football and cricket (see Table 1).

This decline in spectators – an interesting phenomenon to which we shall return – seems common to all advanced countries apart from the United States of America. Certainly football crowds, both in Europe and Latin America, have been declining for two decades, and longer in some countries. Football in England, because of its size and tradition as the country's national winter sport mirrors clearly these difficulties. Attendances at football matches reached record levels in the years immediately after the Second World War. They have been falling steadily ever since, though not always at the same pace, and with occasional reversals of the trend, like the couple of seasons after England won the World Cup in 1966. In 1958–9 33.6 million people passed through the turnstiles: only 16.5 million did so in 1985–6. In fact, 5 million spectators were lost during the 1970s and numbers paying to watch actually fell by 2.75 million during the seasons 1979–81. Players' wages went up by 45 per cent during these two seasons when the cost of living rose by only 20 per cent and by 1981–2, clubs in the third and fourth divisions found their gate receipts amounting to only half of their wage bills.

In such circumstances few clubs made anything but losses. Only twelve out of ninety-two league clubs made a profit in 1982. Credit kept most clubs going, in the form of bank loans, instalment transfer deals and unpaid bills to suppliers. According to the Chester Report,[1] football clubs owed banks £37.3 million at the end of January 1983 and were paying £3 million a year in interest. Clubs lack capital. They do have assets – the ground and the players – but they are not easy to liquidate. Some clubs have sold the ground to the local authority and then leased it back thereby raising a once and for all sum. It is not easy to raise capital by share issues. Dividends are restricted by League rules and the directors want to retain control of the clubs. A few clubs have got round the issue of restricted dividends by forming holding

[2]

companies. But the crux of the matter is that professional football clubs, limited liability companies since the 1890s, have not been in business to make profits for either share-holders or directors. They have aimed for success on the field, which usually brings profits in its wake, but unlike other business ventures they have not been profit maximizers – i.e. making maximum profits is not their primary concern. The satisfaction, and occasionally the financial returns, have come in other ways. But we digress.

As the banks began to follow a less generous policy towards football clubs and as gates fell further, the search for alternative sources of revenue became more urgent. Individual clubs increasingly turned to the world of commerce, to advertising and sponsorship. Competition sponsorship was resisted for some years by both the Football Association and the Football League. Indeed the FA Cup, first competed for in 1871–2, still retains its famous name unsullied by any commercial prefix. But the, National Dairy Council sponsored the Football League Cup during 1982–6 and the Japanese camera and office equipment firm Canon bought the Football League for three years and £3.2 million in 1983–4.[2]

Sponsorship of sport is not new. Aristocratic patronage was important for a variety of sports in the seventeenth and eighteenth centuries, notably in horse-racing, the prize ring, pedestrianism, and cricket. In the nineteenth century, when the modern sporting world was being born, the early sporting press often promoted particular events. Local publicans also offered pitches and accommodation. The *News of the World* was putting up the money for match play golf as early as 1903. Even in the years between the two World Wars, some sports looked to newspapers to meet the expenses and occasionally the cost of prizes for particular events. The *Daily Mail*, for example, sponsored both professional billiards and snooker, and the pristine world of amateur athletics even took money from the *News of the World*, which sponsored meetings, organized its own British Games at the White City, and even sponsored the Oxford and Cambridge athletics clubs matches against American Universities. In addition, companies like Dunlop and Penfold regularly sponsored golf tournaments. But it is since 1963, when Gillette came to the aid of cricket by sponsoring the first one-day restricted overs county knock-out competition, that sports sponsorship has become an industry in itself. In the last fifteen years or so, in particular, its growth has been phenomenal.

It is a growth which cannot be charted precisely. Companies are often reluctant to give details of sponsorship arrangements and sports too are reticent. Accounting procedures also make it difficult to identify what is being spent on what, with money spent on the sponsorship of sport often included in more general company promotional or public relations expenditures. But the estimates show an unmistakable trend. In 1971, for example, £2.5 million was spent on sports sponsorship. By 1982 that figure had grown to £84.7 million and today is thought to be well in excess of £100 million (compared with only £15 million on the arts). Not surprisingly a clutch of specialist agencies has grown up to provide the link between the commercial sponsor and the world of sport. Since 1981 the Sports Council has had a Sports Sponsorship Advisory Service and the Central Council of Physical Recreation its own Sponsorship of Sport Committee. There is also an Association of Sports Sponsors, even an Association of Soccer Sponsors which claims that over 3,000 manufacturing companies have taken part in some form of football sponsorship in the years 1984–6. Our interest lies in two main areas: why the sponsors do it and what this new development means for sport.

Straightforward advertising of local products around grounds or in match programmes is almost as old as organized sport itself. It was a way of catching the collective eye of the crowd and of associating oneself with a local and, with luck, successful and popular phenomenon. It was part of the contribution which a local tradesman or manufacturer could make to the social life of his district. Sports goods makers were obviously among the first to be involved in persuading élite players to use and endorse tennis rackets, cricket bats or football boots in the hope that people would be persuaded to buy the product. The idea that sport was an effective channel through which mass opinion could be influenced is not, therefore, new. But sport is now used for promoting every kind of product and the key to the expansion of sports sponsorship in the last fifteen years is television coverage. What the sponsors can get out of it can be illustrated by the Cornhill Insurance Company's £4.5 million sponsorship of English test match cricket which began in 1980. Before the deal 2 per cent of the population had heard of Cornhill; by 1985 the 'name awareness level' had risen to 20 per cent. From being relatively unknown in 1980 Cornhill became the second most spontaneously named insurance company after the all-mighty Pru. Those 15,000 times when Cornhill Insurance was flashed onto BBC TV screens during the 200 hours of test match cricket in 1985 were having some impact. The company's turnover of just under £100 million in 1977, became £200 million by 1985. The £125,000 which Mita Copiers paid Aston Villa in the 1985–6 season allegedly bought them £4.5 million worth of 'exposure'.

There are other advantages for the sponsor. Some argue that sports sponsorship is the acceptable face of advertising. Sport is a worthwhile activity which many people find attractive. Putting money into sport can be likened to an act of social work – giving something back to the community out of those apparently bottomless profits. Sports sponsorship, in other words, is good for the company's image.

Images, of course, are tricky things to manipulate. Not every company would want to be associated with a sport whose own image is tarnished, either by the behaviour of the players or the spectators. Which sport a company decides to sponsor will vary according to how the company sees its product – at what sector of the market it is aiming. It would be a little surprising if Croft and Co., the purveyors of those fine sherries, suddenly decided to support the Rugby League; but it is not very surprising to find the company backing a series of one-day horse trials.

Anything can be sponsored now, from the kit of an individual football-player to a fence on a three day event course. Sponsors can be multinational companies or small local businesses. Both probably have one thing in common: they are anxious to be associated with success. They want their team, their athlete, their horse or their car to do well and preferably to win, but an obsession with winning can present sport and sponsor with problems.

The goals of sport and commerce are not always identical. In track and field athletics, for example, there will be no shortage of companies willing to sponsor top-class meetings, featuring international champions like Cram, Coe and Ovett. The queue will be nothing like as long for junior meetings with no big-name competitors no television coverage. One inquiry monitored 125 instances of sponsorship of youth sport between 1981 and 1983. But these occasions accounted for only 0.2 per cent of the total spent on the sponsorship of sport. Also, although the sponsoring company will want the attractiveness of the event ensured by the presence of top performers, it may not always suit the training schedules or racing programmes of these athletes – who may, even so, be placed under a lot of pressure to compete. If sponsors can give, they can also take away. When a sponsor decides not to renew, replacements can be hard to find especially for the middle-ranked or up-and-coming sportsman or sportswoman. Much as sponsors may want it, no team or athlete can offer a guarantee of success.

Finally, just as some companies would not wish to be associated with certain sports, so sport might be doubtful about taking money made from the sale of particular products. Tobacco and alcoholic drinks are two obvious products which come to mind. If sport is to be presented as an avenue to personal health and fitness, it can hardly take money from firms who sell goods which have been clearly demonstrated to undermine health and fitness. Cricket was prepared to accept the sponsorship of the tobacco firm John Player for its Sunday League. This suited Player down to the ground. Cigarette advertising on television had been banned and sponsorship of televised Sunday afternoon cricket meant that John Player kept their name before the public ahead of rival manufacturers.

Sponsorship's benefits are clear, but it is also possible that it might undermine the traditional organization and structure of British sport. 'He who pays the piper calls the tune', and the day may come when the voluntary organizational basis of so much top-level sport in this country is imprisoned by business interests. In other words, reliance on business money will make it difficult to stave off business control and values. Top-level sport has always had a business side to it, but the ruthless pursuit of profit has not, generally, been the most important motive. Are the bureaucracies of the individual sports strong enough to resist the pressure when it comes? And what happens, in athletics for example, if the many unpaid voluntary workers decide that they should be paid too?

Prejudice in British sport nowadays boils down to the operation of sexism and racism. As we shall see later it remains true that the poor participate less than the better off in most sports. Class distinction, while not entirely eliminated, has much diminished over the last fifty years, at least so far as playing is concerned, although working people still seem to play little part in administering its higher echelons. But with regard to sexism and racism, as they are endemic in British society, so they are a part of British sport.

At first sight it seems rather implausible to be suggesting that women are still being discriminated against in sport because they are women, when two female javelin throwers can collect fees and appearance money of £10,000 each. Moreover, runner Zola Budd received £90,000 for one race. But sport remains a largely masculine world both at the top and at the bottom. Men play more than women at both levels, and watch more than women. Moreover, it is men who dominate most sport bureaucracies. Women have had to fight for the still unequal place they occupy in today's sporting life.

In fact, at the end of the nineteenth century, sport was as closed to women as were higher education and the leading professions. Sport was considered unsuitable for women. It was not only that it was unfeminine, but it was also alleged to produce physical and mental disorders, a position supported by a good deal of respectable medical opinion. Hockey, for example, was said to inhibit breastfeeding. It was not only men who held such views. Many women shared the idea that their role was primarily domestic, their natures inherently unsuitable for 'manly' physical exertion.

However, as reforming activity began to open up the professions to women and obtain political citizenship for them, so the stereotypes about what was possible in the physical sphere, along with the medical evidence which supported them, were also being challenged. In particular, physical education and games in the expanding girls' public schools and in the universities led to an improvement in women's physical condition, thus, it was argued, enabling greater intellectual achievement as well. The opposition was mostly outflanked. A pioneer of women's physical education, basing her work on the system of drill originated by the Swede Per Henrik Ling, was Madame Bergman-Osterberg. She skilfully adapted fashionable notions about the present and future state of the race. 'I try to train my girls to help raise their own sex, and to accelerate the progress of the race; for unless the women are strong, healthy, pure and true, how can the race progress?'[3] Hockey, tennis and cricket were played by middle-class girls in middle-class schools before 1914, though in clothing which inhibited their freedom of movement as well as stifling the passions of any male spectators.

There is probably no single turning point in the emancipation of the sporting woman. Gains were continually having to be defended and there were plenty of men ready to occupy the last ditch. But as in much else, the First World War loosened old restraints and made a total reversion to the old ways very difficult. In Britain, the war offered new opportunities for young working- and middle-class women to take factory jobs, often away from home and the stern parental supervision which traditionally went with it. Their welfare brought into being almost a new industry whose aim was to provide recreational opportunities in a sober atmosphere. This had the effect, among others, of opening up the field of sport to women. On Tyneside, for example, women's football teams proliferated and appear to have enjoyed a vigorous life up to the General Strike.[4]

Again, it can be no coincidence that it was in 1919 that

Suzanne Lenglen, with her masculine style of play and her radical style of dress, astonished Wimbledon. Gone were the corsets, baggy blouses and petticoats which women had always worn to play tennis. She sported more rational dress, one piece, with a hem-line half-way down the calves.[5]

Women, mainly of middle-class backgrounds, were setting up their own sporting organizations in the 1920s and 1930s. The Women's Cricket Association, for example, was formed in 1926 and the first tour to Australia was undertaken during the British winter of 1934–5. The party included seven teachers, a couple of secretaries and several with no particular occupation; of course, they paid their own fares.

In track and field athletics, women-only meetings were arranged and the first England–France women's international was held before the formation of the Women's Amateur Athletic Association in 1922. They seemed to welcome a (not necessarily equal) partnership with the true blues of the male Amateur Athletic Association. But an odd little episode postponed that particular bonding. The AAA had told the women to form their own association and then apply to them for affiliation. But when they did they were refused! It would be interesting to know what prompted that decision. When the Ladies Hockey Association had similarly tried to join the Hockey Association in 1895 they too had also been refused. At least the women could compete in the Women's World Games, which they did in 1926, 1930 and 1934.

Breaking into the Olympics was no easier than getting into the AAA. Baron de Coubertin, the founder of the modern games, was opposed to women participating in sport. There were no women in the first games of 1896 and only thirty-six in 1908 when they officially competed for the first time, but were restricted to tennis, archery, figure skating and yachting. The British Olympic Committee, however, was impressed by the demonstrations of gymnastics, swimming and diving organized by women to coincide with the London Olympics of 1908 and, after the International Swimming Federation had accepted events for women, the Swedes scheduled swimming and diving for women at the Stockholm

Olympics in 1912. But it was 1928 before the International Amateur Athletic Federation recommended a women's programme of track and field and then only in five events: the 100 metres, 800 metres, 400 metre hurdles, discus and high jump. The British Women's AAA said it was not enough and did not go. It was 1936 when the first British women, ran, threw and jumped in Olympic competition.

Ironically it was the coming of the cold war, together with the entry of the Soviet Union and other eastern European teams into international competition from 1952, and especially their participation in the Olympics, which probably did most to boost women's sport in the West. Russia and the German Democratic Republic in particular won many of their international matches by virtue of the strength of their women competitors. This challenge, together with pressure from women in the West as improved training and preparation led to higher standards, meant that even a group as conservative as the International Olympic Committee (IOC) had to give ground. No women in the Games of 1896 became 518, or just over 10 per cent of the total number of participants, in 1952. By 1976, in Montreal, women were up to 20 per cent, and rather more than 20 per cent of the British team were women. That should be compared with the GDR's team of whom 40 per cent were female. Moreover, the German women won over half their country's gold and silver medals. Indeed they won more medals in Montreal than all the other women in the Games put together.

There is little doubt that the development of sport for women in Britain benefited from the wider movement towards emancipation. But prejudice against women in sport remains. If we look first at the Olympics it is interesting to note which sports and events are still thought by those in authority to be unsuitable for women: boxing, wrestling, weightlifting, judo, football, modern pentathlon, pole vault, the triple jump and the hammer. The fact that there are world championships for women in the modern pentathlon, judo, football and water polo suggests that pressure will continue where it has already begun and soon be initiated where it has been missing so far, to force these events into the Olympic programme. It is as well to remember, however, that it was only in 1949 that the President of the IOC, Avery Brundage, asserted: 'I think women's events should be confined to those appropriate to women, swimming, tennis, figure-skating and synchronized swimming, but certainly not shot putting.' The IOC was still trying to eliminate the women's shot put in 1966. In 1978 they rejected the 3,000 metres. One wonders how far the introduction of rhythmic gymnastics and synchronized swimming is a return to the idea of 'appropriate' events for women. But the clock cannot be prevented from ticking. The key question is how long it will be before the Olympics opens all events to men and women alike.

If opportunities to participate have expanded for women, their presence on many of sports' ruling bodies remains remarkably like their number in the British House of Commons, i.e. not commensurate with their proportion of the population. There are still only three women on the IOC. The Football Association also sets its face against the women's game, a game which had 6,000 players in 278 clubs, mainly in the South of England, at the end of the seventies. The FA has only a token woman on the Council. Not only is women's football considered unseemly by the FA but girls and boys are discouraged from playing the game together in the country's primary and junior schools. The film *Gregory's Girl* was a nightmare the FA are determined will never become reality. It is interesting to note the similarity between British and Soviet attitudes here. The Soviets also consider football an unsuitable game for women because, as their sports leaders have argued, it 'damages organs and arouses unseemly passions'. One reason why women's cricket has grown so slowly has been the lack of encouragement from Lord's. Women cannot play there (they were allowed to once, but it was a concession made with much reluctance and was not repeated until 1987). Nor can they become members of the MCC.

The doors of sport may have been pushed open but it remains doubtful if women receive the same encouragement to play as men do. And one of the reasons must be male preference for 'feminine' women which still inhibits female participation. The perception of sportswomen in newspapers, on radio and television still leans towards sexual stereotyping. Sportswomen are acceptable as long as athleticism is combined with glamour and the conventional beautiful body. If the women are plain and notably muscular they are labelled unfeminine or worse. There remains a reluctance in some quarters to accept female muscle. The introduction of the sex test in 1962 can be explained in part by the existence of such stereotyping.

Class and cultural factors often combine in subtle ways to stiffen the obstacles facing women in sport. Not only are most women football players found in South East England, but it was the South East which John Bale identified as the most dominant in women's track and field athletics. Rowing is a sport firmly based on that region too, so that it becomes less of a surprise to discover that the Amateur Rowing Association's sports director of international competition is a woman. If women's sport is more vigorous in the South East it must be partly a matter of resources. But it is also a matter of class, custom and culture as well. In the North and Midlands, for example, football for women prompts much more cultural disapproval – disapproval which is slow to break down. Of course, the publication and popular dissemination of research emphasizing the link between exercise and good health and, in particular, underlining the fact that regular exercise benefits the female metabolism, makes a contribution towards weakening long-held prejudices. The running and jogging booms and the performance of women marathon runners, with a growing minority running faster than all but an élite of men, has shown that it is not biological frailty which has held women back in the past. Finally, the example of the female athletes of East Germany suggests strongly that it is prejudice of one sort or another which has inhibited the participation of women in British sport. Early selection, careful schooling, rigorous scientific training and a society which provides opportunities for women to engage in other than the more traditional roles are the basis of the athletic success of the East German women. Perhaps when

British women attain similar standards it will be an indication that sexism in British sport has disappeared.

Sport then, has usually meant sport for men. There is a long history of discrimination against women. Similarly it would be difficult to claim that discrimination on grounds of race has been absent in sport.

South Africa is the homeland of segregated sport as is now well known. This was true well before the Nationalists won the election of 1948 and began to establish the formal machinery of apartheid. The South African Cricket Association, for example, was formed in 1890 and was all white. The first cricketers from South Africa to come to England arrived in 1894 having left out of the party T. Hendricks, an outstanding coloured player. The English cricket authorities consistently accepted the racialist nature of cricket in South Africa. When one of the early English teams to visit South Africa, in 1890–1, decided to play a match against a non-white team the amateurs in the touring eleven refused to take part. It was a match never to be repeated until tours stopped seventy-five years later. K. S. Duleepsinhji, a nephew of the great Ranjitsinhji, who had learned his cricket in England and played for Sussex, was chosen for the first test match against the touring South Africans of 1929. The visitors objected and he was not chosen for the remaining four games. Interestingly Duleepsinhji's uncle had also been left out of the first test against Australia in 1896 under circumstances which suggested that his colour might have had something to do with it although it was his eligibility that Lord Harris, the Chairman of Kent County Cricket Club and a recent President of the MCC, was apparently concerned about. None the less, Sir Home Gordon, a cricket historian, claimed that one veteran told him that if it were possible he would have him expelled from the MCC for having 'the disgusting degeneracy to praise a dirty black'. It was a similar picture in Rugby Union and soccer. Roy Francis, the coloured Rugby League player, was not chosen for the tour of Australia in 1946 because it was thought that the host country would object.

In Britain itself discrimination against the non-white sports player was not systematic, unlike the United States of America, for example, where until 1945, top-level baseball, basketball and football barred blacks. They played in their own leagues or not at all.[7] Yet even in Britain there are enough examples of racial discrimination at work in sport to suggest that if there had been a sizeable coloured population before the 1950s and 1960s, the record would have been little different from America's, even if it would have been better than South Africa's. In boxing, for example, a proposed heavyweight contest between the coloured world champion, Jack Johnson, and Bombadier 'Billy' Wells, the British champion, scheduled for the summer of 1911, was not allowed to take place when the owners of the hall took out an injunction against the promoter. The motives for the injunction and the public campaign which surrounded it were that the fight was likely to exacerbate racial tension, not only in Britain itself, but also in the Empire and the USA. A similar excuse was used by the Home Secretary, when forbidding a fight between Joe Beckett and Battling Siki in 1932. Boxing has been particularly adept at promoting a non-racist image but in the 1930s and 1940s the British Boxing Board of Control refused to allow non-whites to challenge for British Championships.

In the Britain of the 1980s – when 4.5 per cent of the population of England and Wales in 1981 lived in households whose head had been born in the new Commonwealth or Pakistan – blacks not only apparently compete equally in all sports, but dominate some of them, or particular events within them. Of the 600 professional boxers in Britain, for example, 30 per cent are black. Similarly, the English athletics team for the last Commonwealth Games contained 33 per cent of athletes of Afro-Caribbean origin, even though their estimated proportion of the population as a whole was only 2 per cent. What does this mean in terms of our theme of racial discrimination in sport? Does it suggest that British sport is presently setting an example to the rest of society by insisting that only ability counts?

There certainly seems to be evidence that blacks themselves see sport as one area where they can succeed. Sport appears to provide the individual with a fair chance. Not only does it have clearly laid down bodies of rules which govern its conduct, but also ability in sport can be seen and measured on scales which are more objective than those applied in other areas of social and economic life. Goals, runs, wickets, times, distances and knock-out blows cannot be fudged.

However, there may be other forms of prejudice at work. Ernest Cashmore (1982), a sociologist, quoted the former Coventry City and currently Tottenham Hotspur footballer, Danny Thomas,

> Initially, to make the breakthrough, it's very difficult for black people. It's the same as the rest of society, if there are two people of equal ability, the white person will usually be given the opportunity.

Research in the United States claims to have provided evidence in support of this belief. In basketball, for example, 'on average a black player must be better than a white player if he is to have an equal chance of transiting from the minor leagues to the major'.[8] Convincing evidence in support of the notion in a British context is hard to come by. But other work in America suggestive of the existence of more subtle forms of discrimination in sport may be more easily transposed to a British context. Although black players dominate American professional basketball and football and are prominent in baseball, their absence from certain important positions on the field is very noticeable and can hardly be accidental. In baseball, for example, the pitcher is the most important player and likewise the catcher is a crucial member of the team. At the beginning of the 1980s only 5 per cent of major league pitchers and catchers were black. Similarly, in football, black running backs, wide receivers and corner backs are ten a penny. But there are few centres or inside linebackers – and almost no quarter-backs. It is the quarter-back who leads the attack on the field, often calling the moves or plays. He is the fulcrum on which the whole team effort turns.

In Britain detailed work of this sort remains to be done. But a quick look at our own professional football game suggests a similar pattern of channelling of black players away from those midfield positions which could be said to be the equivalent of the quarter-back in American football. In 1985–6 in the first division, all those 316 players who took part in fifteen or more league games, including substitutions, were distributed among the three major playing roles as shown in Table 2. The 60 per cent of blacks who were attackers also suggests a racial stereotype that sees black players as better suited to the glamorous and flashy role of the striker. An alternative explanation might be that with a shortage of effective goalscorers, it is less easy to ignore black candidates. It would still be racism at work. The team captain is perhaps also a focal point, the man with extra responsibility who gives orders and takes decisions. There are no black captains in the Football League.

Neither Rugby League nor Rugby Union have many black players at the top level and hardly any, in either code, who play in those crucial initiatory positions around the scrum of scrum half and stand off. In British athletics at the highest level, blacks dominate the sprints for men and women, and the long and triple jumps. This can, no doubt, be partly explained by tradition and the use of American role models like Calvin Smith and Carl Lewis. But it has almost certainly got something to do with the stereotypes which live in the minds of trainers, coaches and managers about 'natural ability' and what black athletes are able to do. Nearly all those trainers, coaches and managers are white.

So there are no black middle-distance runners among the top echelon in Britain. In the same way there are no black tennis players or golfers either. Again the comparison with the United States is interesting. The number of black players in the professional circus which exists in both golf and tennis

TABLE 2: *First division footballers by race and field position 1985–6*

|  | ATTACKERS (%) | MIDFIELD (%) | DEFENDERS (%) |
|---|---|---|---|
| All players | 27.8 | 29.4 | 42.4 |
| White players | 23.3 | 31.2 | 44.9 |
| Black players | 60.5 | 13.1 | 26.3 |

can be counted very quickly indeed. And once the mind begins speculating in this way it is bound to ask why Liverpool and Everton have produced no black players and why the Asian population of the West Riding of Yorkshire has failed to produce even one cricketer to satisfy the, some would say, not particularly demanding standards of the Yorkshire County Cricket Club. If one's gaze is elevated from the confused struggles of the field to the relative calm of stands, office and boardroom then where are the black administrators and officials, coaches and managers, umpires and referees? In America only three blacks have ever managed major league baseball teams in the thirty years or so when that has been theoretically possible.

There is other evidence of racist attitudes in sport, most notably among the crowds. In recent years crowds at boxing, cricket and football in Britain have exhibited hostility towards black men because they are black men. It has sometimes shown itself in abuse of black players on their own team. It is most common in football where chants of 'Ugh, Ugh, Ugh' or 'nigger, nigger, nigger' when a black player is on the ball are commonplace occurrences. Some black players say that such abuse makes them concentrate better and try harder and that success eventually produces acceptance or, at least, resignation. To the observer it seems part of the unacceptable face of football.

Racist remarks fall easily from the tongues of white players, coaches and managers. Again this takes us back to the stereotype we noticed earlier. Football is a hectic, physical contact game where perhaps some things done and said in the heat of an impulsive moment should be and are quickly forgotten. But some stereotypes persist in spite of any amount of contradictory evidence. Two favourite ones among the football cognoscenti are that black players are lazy and they have 'no bottle', in other words, they will avoid the hard, physical challenge which is sometimes necessary to win the ball. Those players who have reached the top in spite of the prejudice say only positive things about it: 'It has provided an additional motivation' is an oft-quoted response. But how about all those other players who did not react in that way but became depressed, embittered and were forced out of the game that might have provided them with a living?

But sport will continue to be a vital cultural interest for many young black people. It may not be a discrimination-free zone in a largely racist society, but it seems to be an area where what you can do counts for more than what you are. 'Inspired by successful black sports stars, encouraged by schoolteachers, who still crudely regard blacks as naturally gifted in sports, and chastened by peers' stories about rampant discrimination in the job market, young blacks seek careers in sport.'[9] The fact that only a small minority make it to the top will no more inhibit young blacks than it did those sports-obsessed working-class whites who saw the chance of fame and riches through sport earlier in this century. Even the majority who do not attain élite status may still obtain much from the experience in terms of excitement, prestige and self-expression. But if it is at the expense of a neglected education and at least partly as a result of racist stereotyping, such enjoyment would ironically lead to a dead end. Unfortunately, there are many people both inside and outside sport only too willing to direct youngsters down this aimless road.

For two weeks in the middle of summer, 1986, the leading sports of America had to share the many pages normally devoted exclusively to them in the nation's newspapers with reports of the deaths of two more athletes from cocaine poisoning. One was a University of Maryland basketball player, the other a member of the Cleveland Browns football team. They were aged twenty-two and twenty-three respectively. These deaths followed closely on the revelations concerning drug-taking among leading basketball players which disfigured the 1985 season. Although it is not always easy to make the distinction, these drugs were not taken to improve directly the performance of the athletes concerned. But one estimate has suggested that about a million American athletes do take drugs to alter their physique and improve their performance. How far has drug-taking become a serious problem in contemporary British sport either to enhance performance or for social and psychological reasons?

It is easier to ask such a question than to answer it. The International Olympic committee, for example, has banned the use of over seventy drugs together with many other related substances. Theoretically the penalties for infringing the rules are unambiguous and severe. In such circumstances neither athletes nor coaches are likely to discuss openly their use of illegal substances. This makes it impossible to say exactly how many athletes take which drugs in what circumstances. Its underground nature also makes it a subject liable to exaggeration and hysteria, particularly in a context in which the problem of drug addiction in the wider society is being identified as a serious social matter.

In the early part of the century it tended to be animals who were doped, notably greyhounds and racehorses. In 1904 the Jockey Club made it an offence to give either stimulants or depressants to a horse and once saliva tests were introduced in 1910 detection was difficult to escape. On the other hand the Report of the Paton Committee on the Scheme for the Suppression of Doping, 1971, emphasized that the doping of racehorses could not be entirely eliminated.

Even the doping of human athletes, however, has a longer history than might be thought. The trainer of the American winner of the Olympic Marathon in 1904 later admitted that he had injected him with strychnine twice during the race. In 1909 the AAA discouraged experiments involving the administering of oxygen to athletes just prior to races. But drug-taking is essentially a post-Second-World-War problem. It probably originated in the highly compititive context of college athletics in California in the late 1950s and spread to the Eastern States and then to Europe from there. Sex tests were introduced in athletics in 1962 and five Eastern European women refused to take them and did not compete in the European championships of that year. The suspicion was that their manly appearance was the result of drugs as well as hard training. The Tour of Britain cycle race was tested for drugs from 1965. But it was only in 1971 that the International Amateur Athletic Federation adopted anti-drug legislation and it was not until 1978 that competitors in the AAA championships were obliged to submit to tests for drugs, following the disqualification of several well-known European athletes the year before. Other sports have been much slower than athletics to react to the problem.

There are four main groups of drugs, three of which are taken for the purpose of improving performance. First are the stimulants, including amphetamines, cocaine and caffeine. They can have the effect of expanding training periods and helping athletes to resist pain as well as improve performance and boost confidence. Synthetic versions of the body's own stimulant, adrenalin, can also be used in preparation for events. The second main group of drugs are narcotic analgesics. Morphine, heroin and methadone are examples. Morphine, for example, not only kills pain but provides a powerful, if short-lived, stimulus. It was often used by cyclists nearing the end of road race stages to counter fatigue and make recovery from physical tiredness more rapid. The third group of drugs which may be taken to improve athletic performance is anabolic steroids. Their use is most noticeable in the sense that they help to build up body fat and muscle quickly, particularly when accompanied by a tough training regimen which they may help the athlete to accept psychologically. The male hormone testosterone contributes to the building up of the body. It can be made easily in the laboratory and taken by both male and female athletes. The diuretic drugs constitute the fourth main group. They are often taken to eliminate traces of other drugs from the body in order to avoid detection. In addition, the use of science and medicine to enhance performance often come close to drug-taking. Training at altitude, for example, increases the blood count and enables the athlete to improve his performance when he returns to sea level. The same result may be obtained by taking out a quart of blood and replacing it shortly before the athletic event. Hormone engineering is thought to have been used to inhibit puberty in some female gymnasts, thereby slowing down the broadening of the pelvis and the development of the breasts.

We do not really know how widely drugs are taken among leading British athletes. All we have are bits and pieces of information. The supporters of snooker were probably astonished to discover not only that at least one leading player had a serious drug problem, but that another admitted to taking beta blockers (a sedative) to steady the nerves and therefore the cue action. Darts players have a fondness for the socially permitted drugs of alcohol and nicotine. Very little is known about drug-taking among footballers, rugby players, cricketers (except in one famous case), tennis players and golfers. It is in the Olympic sports of rowing, swimming, weightlifting, gymnastics and track and field athletics, that it seems most likely that drugs have or might be taken. The AAA first held drug tests at their championships in 1978 and when the winner of the discus declined to take the test he was disqualified. At the time of writing the Association had introduced random dope tests and recently announced that any athlete found taking drugs would be banned from the sport for life. This latter decision shows a firmer attitude than that of both the European and Olympic authorities who have been willing to reinstate athletes suspended after positive drug tests. The use of random testing is in advance of what has happened in the United States where it has so far been successfully resisted by leading sportsmen and their unions. They see it as a violation of individual human rights and therefore an infringement of the Fourth Amendment. American football, for example, still has no mandatory drug-testing machinery even though, as we have noted, players have died from the effects of taking drugs and the use of steroids is thought to be widespread.

In Britain, the Sports Council has declared itself strongly opposed to the use of drugs. It has established a Drug Abuse Advisory Committee, one of whose purposes is to provide information on the therapeutic alternatives to banned substances. There is also a schools' group on drug abuse in sport. The Council has also told Britain's sporting governing bodies that support may be withdrawn from them if they do not organize an acceptable scheme of testing for drugs. It seems increasingly clear that drug control and random testing should be part of the qualifications for membership of the International Olympic Committee.

Drug-taking is not only a matter of seeking an unfair

advantage; it also undermines the whole notion of sport as an aid to health, because drug-taking undermines health, if not in the present, almost certainly in the future. Drugs can probably never be completely eradicated from sport. But as Professor Arnold Beckett, director of the testing unit at the Chelsea College of Science and Technology, said in 1983, 'If we stay on our toes we can develop procedures that will cause the athlete to use smaller amounts of drugs near the competitions, and this will promote fairness and health . . . Consider the alternative'. Random testing is an advance even on that.

If, however, the man or woman on the Clapham omnibus was asked what he or she thought were the main problems facing contemporary British sport it is almost certain that violence would be on the list and probably at the top. Moreover it would be violence among the sporting crowd, and especially the football crowd, which would be identified as the problem.

Violence on the field, though, might also be seen as a perennial sporting difficulty. Violence has always been part of the fabric of some sports. Often animals were on the receiving end and, in certain cases, still are. In boxing it is obvious that the goal is to knock out the opponent, if possible, and that should be violence enough for all save the most rampant appetites. All so-called physical contact sports, in which men or women struggle physically in order to gain possession of a ball or puck, can and do involve hard challenges. The rules were drawn up in part to curb unfair challenges. In the late nineteenth century football and rugby, for example, were thought manly games, part of whose value both to the individual and society was the way they taught the giving and taking of hard knocks. The shoulder charge in football, the low tackle in rugby were part of the essence of those games, especially for those middle-class ideologists who were keen to persuade any doubters of the important role sport was playing in British society. Both football and rugby in late-Victorian times were so rough that some gentlemen expressed doubts as to whether working men, without the benefit of public school education, could take the strain

[22]

without that tell-tale loss of temper. Violence on the field was not unknown even in cricket. Very fast bowling, often bumped or bounced, was more than once employed to intimidate the less-than-staunch. The history of cricket is studded with the serious injuries caused by the contact of a very hard ball with human flesh and bone.

The key question is not whether violence exists on the sports fields of the 1980s, but whether there is more of it than before. Even if there existed a mass of sophisticated statistics relating to violence in sport it would be far from easy to interpret them. Needless to say such data do not exist. Without that kind of evidence it is difficult to be sure that it is change that is being monitored and measured. All that can be offered here is to note a widespread belief that the threshold of sporting violence has risen and offer one bit of statistical, one of observational and two pieces of legal evidence.

The statistical evidence is set out in Table 3 and shows the increase in the number of cautions issued by referees to footballers in the juridical area of the Birmingham Football Association between the 1920s and the late 1970s. Even after several caveats have been made – for example that not all the offences would be for violence and the increased numbers of cautions may in part represent a changed perception on the part of the football authorities rather than a real increase in the number of offences – the numbers are still striking. Certainly the growth in the number of cautions outstripped the growth in the number of affiliated clubs. It is also a fact

TABLE 3: *Birmingham Football Association discipline*

| YEAR | CAUTIONS | AFFILIATED CLUBS |
|---|---|---|
| 1924–5 | 112 | 1,182 |
| 1936–7 | 296 | |
| 1946–7 | 117 | 1,115 |
| 1956–7 | 310 | |
| 1966–7 | 1,233 | 2,424 |
| 1976–7 | 6,666 | c.3,000 |
| 1979–80 | 9,479 | c.3,000 |

*Source*: Minutes Birmingham & District FA 1920–80.

that the shortage of referees is chronic: it might be suggested that the job has become too unpleasant save for a determined and persistent few.

The piece of observational evidence relates to cricket. Fast, short-pitched bowling, at all batsmen, whether the highly skilled men at the top of the order or the no more than semi-skilled batsmen at the bottom, has become so common-place in the last ten years that batsmen now wear helmets and, often, arm and chest protectors. It is a matter of some astonishment that the British cricket establishment has done nothing to remove from the apex of the game such a danger to life and limb. The laws of cricket state that the systematic bowling of fast short-pitched balls is illegal, yet they have never been so systematically bowled. It could be argued that the batsman's helmet has invited rather than discouraged this form of attack.

The courts have recently sat in judgement on two cases of serious violence by one Rugby Union player against another. A Newbridge forward brought a private prosecution against David Bishop, Pontypool's international scrum half, after he had been punched while lying on the ground in a club match in October 1985. Bishop received a month's prison sentence which was suspended on appeal. The Welsh Rugby Union then suspended Bishop for a year, not so much for the assault, but for his persistent denial of responsibility. The Rugby League intimated that Bishop would not be allowed to turn professional until the suspension had been completed. In the same year, a police constable bit off part of another policeman's ear during a game between Cardiff and Newport police teams for which he served a six-month prison sentence. The Bishop case particularly throws light on attitudes to violence within Rugby Union as some people thought it against the game's unwritten code for a player to bring such a case to court.

In Britain, however, contemporary concern about violence on the field has been dwarfed by concern about the behaviour of sporting crowds. The spectators at football matches have been under scrutiny for the last two decades and a new peak of attention followed the terrible incidents at the Heysel

Stadium in Brussels in May 1985 when thirty-nine Juventus supporters died following a charge by Liverpool fans. The coming together of the words 'football' and 'hooliganism' has brought a new phrase to the language, the 'football hooligan'. The phenomenon has produced conflicting interpretations among public, politicians, police, press and sociologists. It has, to date, defied not only all attempts to eradicate it but most attempts to explain it as well.

There have been crowd disturbances at football matches ever since the modern game began about 120 years ago, but that does not necessarily mean that contemporary football hooliganism has clear historical antecedents in the years before the First World War. Let us look briefly at four examples of crowd disturbances at football matches before 1914, two at top-level matches, two in the murky depths of junior football. First, a second-division match between Leeds and Manchester United at Leeds in April 1906. This is how the *Yorkshire Post* of 23 April described the incident.

All the season the spectators (at Elland Road) have been remarkably well behaved, and though with a perfectly natural and legitimate bias towards their own team, ready to recognize and applaud good work by their opponents. On Saturday, owing to the blackguardly conduct of some half dozen spectators (in a crowd of about 10,000) this good character was sadly besmirched. Some of the referee's decisions gave offence to the crowd . . . and the passing unpunished of certain acts by Manchester players which a section of the crowd thought should have been penalized. At the close there was some display of feeling, but except for the conduct of some half a dozen roughs, this was confined merely to vocal disapproval. These few, however, took to the cowardly reprisal of throwing missiles, and one of these struck the referee on the nose, though happily without serious results. The suspension of the Bradford ground, which curiously enough followed on a match with Manchester United, has apparently not acted as a deterrent on the few hooligans who infest all football grounds . . .

[25]

The second example is taken from the *Tottenham Edmonton and Wood Green Weekly Herald* for 24 February 1904 and relates to the FA cup-tie between Tottenham Hotspur and Aston Villa of the previous Saturday. 'The extraordinary scenes which marked and marred the match were altogether strange to Tottenham – we might say to the South – and have shown how absolutely necessary is the exercise of foresight, in providing for actual and would be spectators of a cup-tie.' The gates were closed for the first time in Tottenham's history half an hour before the kick-off. 'The pressure was so great that people had to burst out, first at the Park Lane end, where a number of spectators climbed over the railings surrounding the pitch . . . Then those at the other end did the same and it was here that the crowd got absolutely out of control eventually bringing about the abandonment of the game.' Seat-holders outside the ring could not see when dozens of men stood in front so they stood on their seats and that meant that those behind them could not see. Some climbed on the railings around the ground but all could not do this and as the men at the front did not sit down 'cinders, orange-peel and even a bottle were thrown at them to persuade them to do so'. The game began late and was soon stopped by crowd encroachments on to the pitch. After a 35-minute first half it was decided that in such circumstances it could not be a cup-tie and it became a friendly. When this was announced at half-time, many of the crowd left, others invaded the pitch and the match was abandoned. 'A good deal of horseplay was indulged in within the fences and occasional bouts of fisticuffs occurred, while deliberate attempts were made to further damage the palings. An additional number of police had been sent for and every now and again they ran certain excessively boisterous spirits off the ground . . . Finally the police made a great "drive" and cleared the ground.' Only thirty policemen were engaged inside and outside and later reinforcements brought the total up to 143 altogether. The crowd was 32,000 with many more locked out.

The two examples of crowd disturbances at junior football matches have been taken from the minutes of the

Birmingham and District County Football Association, as it was then called, and chosen because of the rare detail which they offer of the context of the incidents. The first took place in November 1904 during a match between Wednesfield Church and Willenhall Pickwick. Mr Craddock, the referee, wrote to the local football association.

> Play was proceeding very quietly, about five minutes from time, when a fracas occurred among the spectators at one end of the field. A large crowd quickly gathered, and other spectators rushed pell-mell across the field to see what was the matter. Of course, play was stopped in consequence, and, recognizing that the onus of preserving order rested with the home club, I requested the latter players to clear the field, so as to enable the game to be finished. They were unable to do this and with darkness intervening, I was compelled to abandon the match. I might add that none of the players or myself were in any way molested; it was simply the outcome of rival and quarrelsome partisans. Several free fights occurred previous to this, but did not interfere with the progress of play. Neither club could be blamed for what happened, it being one of those unfortunate occurrences which do sometimes crop up to mar the game.

Willenhall were leading 1–0 when the game was stopped. There were no police present as Wednesfield did not anticipate trouble and never had many spectators.

The final example of crowd disturbance is taken from another referee's report, this time of a Junior Charity Shield match between Atherstone Town and Bournville in December 1907: 'At the conclusion of the game I was surrounded by the spectators and mud was thrown at me. After leaving the ground and on my way to the dressing room, I was also struck a severe blow by one of the spectators (who was following me and is known to the committee of the Atherstone club . . .) blacking my eye and cutting my cheek and nose which bled'. There were no police on the ground but the Birmingham FA Committee did not blame the Atherstone club for this 'as nothing had transpired before this

match to make police necessary'. Atherstone were to prosecute two offenders and five others were warned off the
ground. Warning notices were to be posted and police
assistance engaged for all important matches in the future.

These four examples tell us a good deal about the nature of
pre-1914 disturbances at football matches. First of all the
incidents were often the result of home-crowd dissatisfaction
with the performance of the referee and/or the behaviour of
visiting players. Moreover, inadequate dressing-room accommodation, often some distance from the grounds which were
themselves unenclosed, made them easy targets for disaf-
fected partisans. They did not involve fighting between
groups of rival supporters save in one case and that was
characterized as an occasional rather than a regular occur-
rence. The fact that such outbursts were not expected is
further suggested by the low level of policing. There were no
police on the two junior grounds and only thirty ordered for
an important cup-tie which was bound to attract a crowd
well in excess of 20,000. Overcrowding at top football
matches was not uncommon and could lead to pitch in-
vasions and the completion of matches with human touchlines. Uncertainty about ground capacities, commercial
eagerness and inexperience in crowd marshalling were all
contributory factors. As there is nothing so fractious as a
football supporter who has paid his money but cannot see,
confrontation and violence was always likely in such circumstances. Compare those disturbances with the variety witnessed in the 1970s and 1980s. Before 1914, they did not
happen every week. In the last twenty years, they do.
Modern disturbances are also widespread and organized and
involve direct attacks by groups of young, mainly male,
mainly white working-class supporters of one club on a
similar group of supporters of another. They have become a
regular part of the Saturday ritual of football, not only inside
but outside grounds, prompting a massive police presence at
every game in the first two divisions and at important
matches at lower levels. This aspect of the subject will be
returned to later. The point to be made here is that it is not
enough to count, as a group of Leicester sociologists appear to

have done,[10] all the disturbances at football matches which they can find before 1914 in order to demonstrate the continuity of the genre. The context of the incident is all important because only a detailed investigation of it reveals the true nature and meaning of the violence. The evidence is difficult to collect and its interpretation is not without complications, but it seems clear that the violent disturbances at football grounds before 1914 were of a different character from those in contemporary Britain.

There is then the question of the interwar years, and indeed the first fifteen years after the war's end in 1945. In terms of attendances at top level cup and league games these were the years when most of the ground records were established. The Cup Final at Wembley had to be made an all ticket match after 1923 when many would-be spectators broke through gates and clambered over walls to line the touchlines to see Bolton Wanderers beat West Ham United. Significantly there were no reports of fights between rival groups of supporters. Most contemporary commentators and historians agreed that in these years, in spite of large crowds and minimal policing, disturbances were rare. Occasional outbursts were usually the result of anger against the referee or when defeat proved too hard to take. Only one part of Britain, for a period in the 1920s, offered a different pattern which might repay further research. In Glasgow rival brake clubs – groups of supporters of particular teams who drove to matches in hired charabancs – were frequently rounded up by police, taken to police stations and charged with breaches of the peace. Most of them seem to have been focused on the religious sectarian clubs of Rangers and Celtic. For a time in the 1920s police and magistrates appear to have waged a deliberate campaign against the brake clubs' habit of insulting rivals and becoming involved in violence on the streets. How far these activities were provoked by the draconian Scottish anti-drinking laws is not clear.[11] Apart from that, disorderly behaviour by football crowds was a phenomenon found in those parts of the world – Spain, Italy, Latin America – to which the game had recently and rapidly spread. It was there, after all, that the playing areas began to be fenced off from the spectators. It was there that moats began to be built around pitches. British soccer tourists often commented with an amused, if slightly patronizing superiority, that it would never happen at home.

But in the 1960s it did. There was no single moment which can be pinpointed as when it all began. By the middle of the 1960s groups of young men began to gather together, usually behind the goals at particular ends of grounds, in support of the big city clubs. They also regularly travelled to away matches. Vandalism on British Rail football specials was an early sign of the new phenomenon. It was accompanied by obscene chants and raucous choruses in which new words were adapted to old songs. Groups of fans began to march to the ground together. Fighting with rival groups spread from inside the ground to outside, from during the match to before and after. Vandalism on opponents' grounds, in shops close by and on public transport was apparently exacerbated by the emergence of skinhead gangs among some working-class youths at the end of the 1960s. It was in 1968 that the first investigation and report on 'football hooliganism' indicated that there was a phenomenon which was being identified as a social problem. This was by John Harrington, a Birmingham psychologist. In fact the government had already set up their own investigation and the Lang Report was published in 1969.[12]

Lang felt that more seats and less standing on football grounds would help eradicate the problem. But there must also be closer co-operation between football club and police so that policing could be made easier. Police should be stationed on the terraces and there should be detention centres on the ground. By the early 1970s, the containment of football hooligans was in full swing. Police numbers at matches soared, specially trained snatch squads tried to pick out ringleaders and other offending individuals inside grounds, young away fans were escorted from transport to ground and back and, on the ground, spectator segregation was increasingly applied. Governments took a series of initiatives and the 'problem' was regularly 'solved'.

In 1973, for example, magistrates were encouraged to

impose the maximum level of fine, £100. Police began to use mobile cameras to detect the offenders. Fences around the playing area began to go up in 1974. Cardiff City even introduced identity cards for the under-seventeens. In 1975 a Labour MP said that arrested hooligans should automatically spend a night in gaol and that was the year when the Minister of Sport suggested that alcoholic drinks should be banned on trains and coaches taking supporters to matches. British Rail subsequently suspended their cheap fares for football excursions. In 1977 the Government expressed the view that attendance centres should keep the convicted hooligan away from the scene of his crime on Saturday afternoons. The supporters of some clubs, Manchester United and Chelsea, for example, were banned from travelling to away games during the 1970s. By the late 1970s, not only had at least three young supporters been killed in violence around football matches, but British supporters had fought opponents and police abroad: Tottenham supporters in Rotterdam in 1974, Leeds supporters in Paris in 1975 and travelling supporters of England during the European championships in Italy in 1980. In London, particularly, there was some evidence that the National Front was trying to direct football violence against blacks, especially those employed on the tubes and buses.

For Mrs Thatcher, of course, it is a social order issue. It is part of that collapse of authority and discipline which she likes to date from the permissive sixties and for which a penal response is the only proper one. We shall return to this point in a moment because it is here that disorder at sporting events in general, but football matches in particular, fits into important wider contemporary social and political concerns.

First, we need to ask who the football hooligans are and what their activities mean, both for themselves, and the rest of society. The first question is relatively easy to answer. Research by the Leicester Group in particular seems clear on this point. Football hooliganism is not confined to a fixed deviant minority of working-class youths. It is something sampled by a proportion of the white, male, working class in the 13–30 age group. They are mainly from the lower end of the class, living on the rougher council estates, ill-educated, in poorly paid jobs with few prospects, or, frequently, since the expansion of the recession at the end of the 1970s, having no work at all. They inhabit a culture in which fighting and hardness bring status and reputation. It is a very masculine culture. This image may require some modification in the light of recent suggestions that some of the more violent and organized groups may have more comfortable backgrounds. Young men, in work, from the more affluent working class, dressing in the fashionable casual style and giving themselves ego-boosting titles such as the Anti-Personnel Firm (attached to Chelsea FC) or the Inter City Firm (West Ham) have allegedly been responsible for recent outbreaks of violence which often began in the seats rather than on the well-policed standing terraces.

Any attempt to discover the meaning and purpose of these activities involves entering more controversial terrain. Two explanations in particular have provoked a good deal of public discussion. The work of Peter Marsh and his colleagues, based on close observation on the terraces of Oxford United, then a third division team, in the mid-1970s, emphasized the ritualistic nature of football violence. The function of the 'aggro', or aggravation, was to indicate the participants' membership of what he called 'micro-cultures' or small groups which were important in moulding individual identity. Hence it looked more dangerous than it was. Few blows actually got home and few people were hurt. It was an acceptable way of 'socializing' an aggression which, if repressed, might find more serious forms and targets. The same kind of social anthropological explanation was recently offered after the outbreak of fighting between supporters of West Ham and Manchester United on the Dutch ferry, the *Köningen Beatrix*. Again it was a ritualized struggle with the limits clear and the rules known. Few were hurt. It was done for fun and excitement. 'Escaping momentarily the monotony, powerlessness, and bland normality of the factory-floor or the dole queue, they had experienced a transcendent moment of community with their mates and excitement in the face of danger.'

The second attempt at explanation involves the notion of 'deviancy amplification'. The sequence of events begins with a particular act of rule-breaking, in this case, violence in the football crowds. This is followed in quick succession by three further stages: a shocked social reaction, the labelling of the offenders as deviant, and the ostracism of severe punishment for those apprehended. The whole phenomenon is exaggerated by the response of an alarmed public and especially by the sensationalist attitude of newspapers and television. Not only does such a response make the condemned behaviour more attractive to the potential hooligan but it creates a social problem where one did not really exist. The erection of fences and the institution of strict supporter segregation, for example, merely institutionalize the problem. For Stan Cohen, the football hooligan is one of a series of folk devils 'created' by 'society' in the context of a 'moral panic'.[13]

At the core of both these descriptions of the football hooligan and his relation to society lies a suggested remedy: that society should be so conducted that by means of humane living and social conditions, people develop as beings who are conscious of the rights of others and willing to accept their living space, instead of antagonistically seeing them as a challenge, something to defeat and frighten away. It is a position which has found little favour with either the football or political establishments. They think largely in penal terms. The reaction to the football hooligan has been very similar to the response to civil unrest in the inner cities.

Meanwhile, many working-class people who live close to football grounds do not look forward to Saturday afternoons from August to May. There is a chance that either they will be assaulted or their property damaged. Even if the odds against this happening to them personally are long, they *feel* menaced, especially the elderly and ethnic minorities. Transport workers, on the London underground, on British Rail and on the buses, often have to bear the brunt of football supporter violence. This situation has been exacerbated by Government spending cuts putting pressure on British Rail and London Transport to introduce single-man operation on trains, buses and stations, thereby making them that much more vulnerable to assault. Violence at football matches undoubtedly contributed to the fears which produced working-class votes for a Conservative Party pledged to a law and order policy and the strengthening of the State in 1979 and 1983. It was part of a context in which police numbers and powers were continually being extended. An erosion of civil liberties for hooligans and non-hooligans alike has been one result. Supporters are sometimes evicted because they look as though they might cause trouble and they are standing on that part of the terraces from which trouble habitually comes. 'Away' supporters may have to wait inside their cages for some time after a match is over before police herd them off to coaches or trains.

Except at Luton Town in 1986–7, that is. Visiting supporters were banned from the ground at the start of the season as a Government-favoured membership card scheme was introduced by the club, whose chairman is now a Conservative Member of Parliament and staunch supporter of Mrs Thatcher. Only supporters living within twenty miles of the stadium automatically qualified for a card. Many objections were raised against the scheme both inside the Football League and out, mainly on the grounds that if applied nationally it could be easily circumvented and that it infringed the freedom of movement of the law-abiding spectator.

As for the game itself, it cannot be said to have emerged well from its period of troubles. Neither the Football Association nor the Football League has supplied any leadership. They have responded to physical violence with violence of the tongue. There have been some feeble attempts to improve the game's image and to make it more attractive to the middle class and to family groups. Coventry City, for example, without consulting the club's supporters, converted the Highfield Road ground to seating only in 1981–2. The fans of Oxford United, Leeds United and Sheffield Wednesday quickly demonstrated the advantage to which the resourceful hooligan could turn seats. The move may have attracted more families, but it certainly led to large-scale desertions by the traditional supporters, who preferred to stand and resented paying for a seat they did not want. By 1985–6 the seats were gone and the terraces back at one end of the ground. An ex-schoolteacher persuaded the Football authorities and the National Dairy Council to subsidize a new organization – Soccer As Family Entertainment (SAFE) – not apparently being aware that football traditionally had nothing to do with either families or entertainment. Family enclosures have sprung up everywhere. Unaccompanied adults hate to go there, surrounded by groups of uncontrollable falsettos with doting parents looking fondly on. Football, in spite of the puny attempts of a few clubs to involve supporters more directly, remains wedded to the notion that they should only be seen and heard – and behaving respectably at that – on matchdays. Neither the FA nor the League has produced any long-term educational programme designed to help the young supporter cope with either his ritualized identification or his partisanship.

In the short term, there is little to be hoped for. Football hooliganism will not go away and ordinary people will need to be protected from the depredations of fighting gangs or menacing individuals. That will mean a continued police presence on match days with all the unpleasant paraphernalia of supporter segregation and surveillance. But more thought needs to be given to the whole issue of prevention. In the long term, policies are required which provide improved education and more jobs, with better prospects to take the edge off frustration and the poverty and ignorance which produces it. It is salutary to be reminded that lawless behaviour by young males is not confined to the vicinity of football grounds. The 14–20 age group contains the highest level of offenders cautioned or found guilty of indictable offences. In 1984, 75 per 1000 of this age group in the population were offenders compared with 14 per 1000 of males over 21. It is not easy to see what substitute for fighting, which will offer similar excitement and solidarity to young men, can be found without an improvement and some restructuring of gender behaviour as well as in the material base. It remains an area in which it is difficult to cultivate optimism.

# 2
# Historical development

## 1 Amateurs and professionals

Most people who have played any sport in the last two centuries in Britain have been amateurs. They have not devoted any period of their lives to the full-time preparation for, study and performance of a particular sport. Neither have they received any payment for playing, although other material advantages may have come their way. Sporting ability has, in many cases, gained preferment for those who have possessed it, at least from the eighteenth century when runners and cricketers, for example, were often given positions by aristocratic masters. Later preferential admittance to the ancient universities and jobs for the Blues were commonplace. From the late eighteenth century, however, professional sportsmen began to appear, most notably in cricket, pedestrianism and prize fighting. By the second half of the nineteenth century, the professionals were attracting the attention of those sporting clubs and associations which middle-class gentlemen were setting up in an attempt to organize, rationalize and control both individual events and sports.

Defining an amateur in order to be able to recognize a

professional proved a tricky business in all sports and produced dramatic upheavals in some. As early as 1835, *Bell's Life*, the leading sporting paper of the day, asserted that no one who was a waterman or rowed for a living could be considered an amateur in that sport. Thirty years later the Henley Regatta Committee went further by stipulating that no man could be an amateur oarsman who was or had been by trade or employment for wages, a mechanic, artisan or labourer. One can see that it might be felt that working on the river provided an oarsman with a competitive advantage. On the other hand, it is hard to believe that class prejudice was not in operation too. For one thing Henley maintained their sternness for such a long time. In 1920, for example, admittedly before he had become Grace Kelly's father, John Kelly was banned from competing there because he had been a bricklayer. He was the Olympic sculling champion at the time. Again, in 1936, the Australian Olympic Games eight were excluded from Henley because they had jobs, as policemen as it turned out. The impact of snobbery and exclusiveness here, as in other aspects, is clear.

Meanwhile the staking out of the boundaries between amateur and professional continued to provide mental and emotional exercise for the solidly upper-class organizers of athletics. In particular the exclusive London-based Amateur Athletic Club declared, in 1866, that an amateur was any person 'who has never competed in an open competition, or for public money, or for admission money, and who has never at any period of his life taught or assisted in the pursuit of athletic exercises as a means of livelihood'. Unfortunately 'or is a mechanic, artisan or labourer' was added in 1867, and in 1868 the club came right out with it: the definition began with the clear statement that 'an amateur is any gentleman'. But such grand exclusiveness could not be maintained as track and field athletics grew in popularity in the North and the Midlands. The clubs formed there were all for amateurism but definitely not for the exclusion of those working men who made up some of their most talented members. When the Amateur Athletic Association was formed on the initiative of three members of the Oxford University Athletics club in

1880 the rule excluding mechanics, labourers and artisans from competitions run by the Association was abandoned. But outright professionalism was firmly outlawed.

At about the same time, the Football Association, also heavily staffed by southern ex-University men and based firmly in London, was doing the same. It was 1882 when the FA specifically forbade payments to players for other than genuine expenses and wages lost through taking time off work to play. Cricket, of course, had long had a subordinate niche for its professionals. As in golf, the professional in cricket had a recognized teaching role. This was true not only in the public schools and Oxford and Cambridge, but also in the wealthier clubs. Professional bowlers had long been employed to provide batting practice for gentlemen club members who required it. The crucial moment which determined who should control the great national game of cricket had probably come towards the end of the 1860s with the collapse of the professional touring elevens. Henceforth the authority of the MCC and the county clubs was to be unchallenged. Golf and horse-racing were also well in control of their professional element. For football and rugby, however, the crisis was at hand and eventually the ruling bodies took opposite views on what should be done about the professional.

By the middle of the 1880s both football and rugby had become spectator sports, especially in the Midlands and the North of England. Competitive cup football in particular drew large crowds prepared to pay their pence to stand or sit. In such circumstances it should have occasioned no surprise that team managements were tempted to identify and secure, by a variety of inducements, the best available players for their teams. Opposition to professionalism was not entirely a monopoly of the South, but its most implacable adversaries were located there. Clubs and players were suspended in the first half of the 1880s and it was clear that a breakaway of northern clubs who saw nothing wrong in professionalism was imminent. It was at this tense moment that the FA and most notably its Secretary, Charles Alcock, made one last effort to effect a compromise. A series of meetings in 1884–5 eventually produced an agreement to legalize profession-alism, but under strict controls. Residential qualifications were to be tough and, a little later, a maximum wage together with a retain and transfer system gave the profes-sional clubs – with their limited liability, shareholders and boards of directors – extensive power over their players.

The Rugby Union, on the other hand, was prepared to see any breakaway clubs damned first rather than have anything to do with the paid player. When the crisis arrived in 1895 there was no compromise. A group of twenty-one northern clubs who wished to pay their players broken time payments (for time lost at work) failed in their attempt to win over the Rugby Union. They seceded and set up the Northern Union, which changed its name to the Rugby League in 1922. It is ironic that the new body was itself opposed to out-and-out professionalism and in 1898 introduced a rule stipulating that the players must follow a legitimate calling and not simply be professional rugby players. It also named some vocations that it did not consider legitimate, such as billiard markers, pub waiters and rugby-club employees, and before 1914 the rule was vigorously applied. Even today, the Rugby League is largely part-time and also has a large amateur section whose players play for recreation. The geographical strength of the game has remained in Lancashire, Yorkshire and Cumbria and the hostility of the Rugby Union to it is remarkable in its rectitudinal consistency.

Several factors lay at the root of these conflicts over whether a small élite minority of players in a game should be paid in order that they could either afford the necessary leave of absence from work or become full-time practitioners of a sport. There were undoubtedly some gentlemen who were reluctant to play with working men, professionals or not, but the evidence suggests that they were a declining group and perhaps never very numerous. On the other hand, the professional was subjected to moral pressure. Could he be trusted to 'play the game'? The objection was not so much to actual betting on sport: after all gentlemen pedestrians and cricketers, riders and rowers had often indulged in sometimes sizeable flutters. But gentlemen could be trusted to continue to *try*: they would not throw a race in order to achieve a coup with the bookmaker. When you gambled on a match between gentlemen at least you knew it was honest sport. Could you say the same for the pro? Rational opponents of professionalism, then, tended to fall back on three main arguments.

First, that in team games, like football and rugby, it would inevitably lead to the poaching and buying of players by the larger clubs. This would undermine the local and regional loyalties on which such games had grown up and prospered.

Second, and more important, to allow professionalism would be to encourage an élite of players who would eventually, and sooner rather than later, by virtue of their full-time attention to practice and physical conditioning, outclass the amateur player to such a degree that there would 'be no competition between them'. The amateurs would drop out of the best teams and the top championships. They would either be relegated to a second-class status or give up playing altogether. Either might have serious implications for the grass-roots level of play and might well undermine the contribution of the sport to British social life, which was thought by many enthusiasts to be of great importance. Of course this was to overlook the advantage which the gentleman of leisure had held over those who had to work for a living. He could devote a higher proportion of his time and resources to training. Moreover he was not tired out by heavy labour. That merely opened up another set of problems about the amount of practice and training that was legitimate in what was supposed to be a recreation. As someone once said to Herbert Spencer, to play too good a game of billiards indicated a misspent youth.

Finally, football and rugby, for example, were energetic, physical contact sports. Although both had sophisticated organizations with a central, national headquarters together with regional and local branches, there was a minimum of formal rules. Could such games continue without the acceptance by the players of a series of conventions and unwritten pieces of etiquette which were learned at public school and perhaps even at the grammar schools? It was doubtful if they were learned at the elementary schools and, even if they were, how could a professional, whose livelihood might depend on the outcome of a match or race, be expected to observe them? It was doubtless difficult enough for the gentleman . . .

How far did the effects of professionalism bear out the anxieties of the pessimists? Certainly in football, for example, professionalism did lead to the best talent being monopolized by the clubs who were able to pay for it, but the maximum wage, the retain and transfer system and a buoyant market for spectator sports in general and football in particular from around 1885 to 1955, prevented too great a concentration of wealth and power until relatively recent times.

Was the amateur player forced out of sport at its highest level? In some sports the two groups were kept well apart and did not compete against each other. Boxing, for example, had an amateur world and a professional one with a good deal of one-way traffic from the one to the other. Athletics, in the form of the AAA, dealt very severely indeed with any signs of professionalism. During the two decades before 1900 they prosecuted several professionals who had pretended to be amateurs for fraud. The courts sent convicted athletes to prison, sometimes for six months with hard labour. In 1882 the AAA refused to allow Walter George, the leading amateur middle distance runner of the times, to run against William Cummings, the leading professional. Professional athletics, after 1918, was concentrated in a few events, like the Powderhall Sprints, in a small number of places, such as Scotland and the North of England. By 1900 professionals in other sports were not allowed to compete in amateur athletics meetings. Swimming clubs refused to countenance direct competition between amateurs and professionals. Tennis was rather similar though even more exclusive. A small group of professionals, making the most of their income from coaching and teaching, were kept well away from the All-England Club, the Lawn Tennis Association and the major championships. In spite of such strictness, by the 1920s it would have been impossible to win Wimbledon while just being home on leave from the Ceylon tea plantation, as the second winner did in 1878. But Wimbledon did not allow professionals to play until 1968.

In other sports, most noticeably football and cricket, amateur and professional players could play with and against each other. Certainly, in football, amateurs found it increasingly difficult to find places in an England team dominated by professionals. The last amateur to play in a full international against Scotland, for example, did so in 1911. The days when Mr Topham could 'kindly consent' to play for the Wolves, as he did in 1895, were certainly over by the First World War. Even if a gentleman had the time and the resources, it would not have been socially acceptable for him to have played football in the professional league and it was increasingly difficult to contemplate it without a professional's training routine. The Football Association instituted a separate knock-out cup competition for amateur teams in 1894 which lasted for eighty years. A group of southern clubs did break away to form the Amateur Football Association in 1907 but they crept back to the FA in 1914. The whole question of what constituted an amateur and, particularly, who was eligible to play in amateur internationals, bedevilled relations between the FA and the Fédération International de Football Associations throughout most of the interwar years.

Cricket was rather different. The top amateur players did have the time to play and practise and develop their skills to a similar standard to the professionals, certainly before 1914. This was where the myth of cricket being more than just a game came in. Even after the First World War amateur cricketers were prominent in the county championship. In 1930, for example, there were 219 professionals and 156 amateurs (41 per cent); and even in 1952, 22.5 per cent of first-class players were amateurs. In both years they were heavily concentrated in the southern counties of Essex, Kent, Hampshire, Surrey and Middlesex. It is also worth noting that of the seventeen first-class counties in 1952, only Warwickshire and Sussex had a professional captain. The captaincy of Middlesex was shared by Denis Compton, a professional, and W. J. Edrich, an amateur, and that of Sussex reverted to an amateur in 1953. Of course much of this amateurism was of a less than purist kind. W. G. Grace was allowed to receive £8,835, the product of three testimonials collected for him in 1895, and remain an amateur. This was in contrast to the treatment of the captain of the Welsh International Rugby fifteen, Arthur Gould. When he was about to retire in 1897 he was presented with £600 and the International Board of the Rugby Union declared that recipient and donors had both indulged in an act of professionalism. Fortunately an open vote of members of the Rugby Union later agreed to make an exception. Generous expenses, sympathetic employers, paid journalism and paid positions in the administration of the county clubs enabled cricketers, of whom it might have been more honest to acknowledge their professional status, to retain the privileges of the amateur, such as 'Mr' before his name, and perhaps a separate dressing room and a separate entrance to the ground, although these were gradually disappearing in the 1930s. Cricket was less sectarian about amateurism in some ways than, say, as the Gould case indicates, Rugby Union, but it could be argued that even today, when the élite are all players and the MCC have relinquished power to the Test and County Cricket Board, the same power bases of public schools and Oxbridge still rule the roost.

Did the spread of professionalism discourage the amateur player from playing at all? It is true that part-time players found it increasingly difficult to match the standards set by the full-timers, whether amateur or professional. But the phenomenal growth of participation in all sports in the twentieth century showed that those early fears about the obliterating impact of professionalism were unfounded.

But the other major anxiety expressed by the anti-professional lobby – about professionals 'playing the game' – requires more careful appraisal. Has the spirit of sport inevitably been eroded by its domination at the élite level by the paid performer who has not only a psychological need for victory but a material one as well? It is a subject to which we must return in our concluding section. Suffice it to say at this point that the dominant sporting ideology in the late Victorian and Edwardian periods, perhaps 1870–1914, was that of fair play and the joy of taking part. That was an ideal, of course, which not even all middle-class sportsmen always achieved. In any event there could often be lapses. W. G. Grace, for example, certainly ignored the spirit of cricket when it suited him, as did those pole vaulters at the 1899 AAA championships who refused to lend the favourite a pole after he lost his on the railway. Certainly many working-class sportsmen seemed to be attached to winning. But perhaps the most accurate summary of the pre-1914 and pre-1939 attitude would be that you should give your opponent the fairest of fair play but go in for winning. The difficult questions are how far that has changed in the last thirty years and whether the professionals can be blamed. Certainly few would claim that the current dominant sporting ideology places participation above winning. The cult of success is worshipped in media far more powerful and penetrating than existed before 1939. 'The professional foul' – a phrase, one suspects, invented by a journalist – seems to imply that some infringements of the rules, deliberately carried out, are to be justified as part of a professional code. Professional fouls tend to provoke imitation by the lesser breeds without the TV coverage. Perhaps the really destructive side of 'profession-alism', in the team games at least, is its obsession with trying not to lose rather than going for the win.

In any event, to blame the professional for the ideological shift and to blame only the professional hardly seems fair play. Professionals have, after all, been practising their craft in a society which has traditionally seen the biggest rewards go to the winners in the world beyond sport. Moreover, as we noted earlier, much of the money in modern British sport comes from commercial sponsorship and that money is always seeking out winners.

Some sociologists might say that old amateur/professional distinctions are meaningless today. Professionalism is an attitude of mind: it has nothing to do with distinctions of social class or earning money. Full-time sportsmen will claim that they are all professionals now, and claim it with pride. What they probably mean is that they prepare with thoroughness and perform with determination. The aim is efficiency, an efficiency measured in wins, titles, records, runs, goals or wickets. It is achieved by taking the minimum of risks. The working man's search for security, translated into sport, means trying to make fewer mistakes than your opponent. Only the Rugby Union and the Warsaw Pact countries stand out against professionalism and the conflicts over South Africa may soon leave only the latter.

Our leading athletes, however, retain an amateur status. The professional runners, throwers and jumpers who jog around the Highland Games circuit in Scotland with small money prizes such as £50 for a win are categorized as professionals and therefore not allowed to compete with Coe, Ovett, Cram *et al.* when *they* can earn as much as £10,000-12,000 for one appearance. In 1983 the International Amateur Athletics Federation agreed that amateurs could earn money from their efforts in track and field so long as it was paid into a trust fund. The money could be used for training and living expenses, liberally interpreted, and any surplus could be given to the athlete when he or she retired from the sport. The fund is administered by the British Amateur Athletics Board. The Board pays appearance money, and all contracts which the athletes may sign for the endorsement of products, for example, have also to be ratified by the BAAB. All this, and the retention of amateur status! It seems a strange business. The excuse for it is that it has all come very suddenly for everyone as the result of sponsorship and worldwide television combined. Gently does it, particularly as the countries of the Warsaw Pact do not like individuals receiving money direct: that is the route for defection to the fleshpots of the West. The State will control anything that is coming to them.

So although the old class conflicts surrounding who was or who was not an amateur are buried in the past, the amateur/professional controversy lives on in British and indeed world sport in another guise. The vast majority of active sportsmen and sportswomen are amateurs in the old sense. They may play what they play for a variety of reasons but material reward is not one of them. They are hardly an endangered species but it is not clear that they are receiving an equitable share of the resources which this country devotes to sport. In the past, committees were set up to inquire into professionalism. The Central Council for Physical Recreation now has one looking into amateurism. Not only does that suggest a shift in the structure of British sport, it also provides a measure of the important place sport has come to occupy in the dominant culture of Britain.

### 2 Sport and the media

The relationship between sport and the media has always been an important one. In the middle of the nineteenth century both sport and the transmission of news about it went through a transformation. For newspapers, the steam press, the electric telegraph and the end of state taxes meant that news could be collected, hundreds of thousands of copies could be rapidly and cheaply reproduced and distributed by railway to the most populous parts of the kingdom. Sport began to take on its modern shape once it became a central part of the curriculum of the public schools. It was their products who gave it its rules and staffed its national and many of its local organizations. They and their lower middle-class imitators were sporting evangelists who took their enthusiasms and skills to the people, a people who already had a liking for sporting diversion, though of a relatively rude and coarse kind. It was that liking that had to be brought up to date by playing the same games according to the same rules as their betters. The press was crucial in the process: advertising and publicizing, promoting, even sponsoring and emphasizing a sporting world with its own seasons, festive and holy days.

The first newspaper to mark this growth of sporting news was *Bell's Life in London*. When it began in 1822 it was not a sports-only paper but, as the title suggests, concerned with the goings-on of the capital's rich and fashionable set. But the focus gradually shifted to sporting news though it was still including some non-sporting news in the 1860s. By that time, with a circulation probably in excess of 30,000, it was

bringing profits to its owner of an estimated £10,000 a year.
The fact that only gentlemen could write for it helped to
create a reliable reputation which made it the ideal stake-
holder for prize fights and upper-class bets. It appeared on
Sundays until the 1860s but late in that decade, in an attempt
to match the growth in sport and the increase in public
interest, it began to come out on Wednesdays and Saturdays
instead. The new schedule could not be sustained in the face
of growing competition. *Bell's* monopoly was challenged in
1859 by what became the *Sporting Life*. The new paper
concentrated on the turf but also looked at other sports and
did it for a penny against *Bell's* fivepence. By 1860 the
*Sporting Life* was claiming a circulation of 260,000 and the
ability to publish the details of any sporting championship
within twelve hours of the event. Certainly it carried more
and more varied advertising than *Bell's*. The competition was
increased by the emergence of the *Sportsman* in 1865 and, in
Manchester, of the *Sporting Chronicle* in 1871. The early 1880s
saw Britain possessed of four sporting dailies, *Bell's* having
tried to keep up with the competition by emulating it. It
could not last and it was *Bell's* who went under, the name
being sold to the *Sporting Life*.

By the mid-1880s the British public were supporting three
sporting daily newspapers. Moreover all of them had been
sporting papers from their inception, noticing very little other
news, apart from the stage. They also shared a heavy
concentration on horse-racing which by the 1880s was
taking place somewhere in Britain on almost every day of the
year. But other sports were far from neglected. Finally they
all promoted and sponsored sport as *Bell's* had done, holding
stakes, and providing judges, referees and trophies, sporting
annuals and guides, especially important in the early days of
modern sport when all these elements were rare. Finally they
were all national, even if one was published in Manchester,
and at a penny they were aimed at the masses, rather than
the classes which had been *Bell's* main audience.

There was a weekly sporting press too, which late in
Victoria's reign was expanding in variety and quality. Not all
of these papers had long and profitable lives but two were

especially distinguished and successful. The *Field* became the bible of the hunting, shooting and fishing fraternity. Nor did it ignore the turf. Even ball games had their coverage gradually expanded. The *Field* was a very successful family business. Beginning in 1853, it showed a steady decline of profits after 1890, but the £75,000 made in that year on a circulation of 19,000 (but a much greater readership, of course) shows what thirty-two pages of advertisements aimed at gentlemen could achieve and it remained healthy enough.

The *Athletic News*, on the other hand, was equally successful but very different. It was sporting news without the horse-racing and the betting. It had begun in 1875 in Manchester with the aim of bringing the sporting activities of amateurs to the notice of a wider, mainly northern, public. But as football grew in popularity and professional matches began to attract large crowds, the paper moved with the times, concentrating on football and rugby in winter and cricket and athletics in summer, while finding space for most other sports. In 1887–8 it became a penny paper and its concentration on league football boosted its circulation to 180,000 a week from September to April. From 1893 to 1900 its editor, J. J. Bentley, was also President of the Football League which helped to make the paper the voice of the professional game. In barely a decade it had secured a special position in the minds of those sport-conscious clerks and skilled workmen from the Midlands and the North of England who probably made up the bulk of the readership. Other examples of successful weekly sports papers included *Pastime*, 1883–95, based on London and devoted to the propagating of amateur sports, and *Cricket*, 1880–1914, whose editor for a time was Charles Alcock, Secretary of Surrey County Cricket Club, which gave it a semi-establishment point of view.

What appears to have undermined the specialist sporting press was the increasing attention paid to sports news by the morning, evening and Sunday newspapers. Sporting news was one of those items which proprietors thought helped to sell papers and a sign of this was the emergence of the sports page, increasingly pages, almost universally by 1900. In daily papers sport occupied 10 per cent, and sometimes more, of the available space, as it did from the first issue of the halfpenny *Daily Mail* in 1896. Even the *Daily Herald* ran a sports page, although it tried to draw the line at racing tips which would encourage its largely working-class readership to bet. It is true that the more establishment papers treated sport with a shade more circumspection. *The Times* was prepared to honour with its notice what had mysteriously become great national events, like the Derby and the University Boat Race, but it had no sports editor before 1914, employed no tipster and generally looked down its aristocratic nose at sports with large spectator followings like football and what was to become Rugby League – although cricket was another matter.

But not surprisingly, with Sunday following the Saturday afternoon which, by 1880, had generally ousted Saint Monday as the working man's playday, it was the Sunday press which took up sport's dramatic story with enthusiasm. Some Sunday papers were actually set up to specialize in Saturday's results. The *Referee*, for example, was, in 1877, probably the first Sunday newspaper to run a football results column. The *Umpire* from 1884 and the *Sunday Chronicle* from 1886, also set out to exploit the sporting obsessions of a working class that was still hardly buying a daily paper regularly but was dramatically boosting the circulation of the Sundays and projecting their owners into the plutocratic class. The *News of the World* devoted 14 per cent of space to sporting news in 1895 with cricket, football and athletics usually being given more prominence than horse-racing.

A further competitor in what was becoming an increasingly crowded field was the local evening paper. First with the racing results in the week, it could also offer a results service second to none in immediacy via its football specials which appeared early on Saturday nights soon after the matches were finished. *Saturday Night* in Birmingham must have been one of the first in 1882; four pages for a halfpenny and 'everything readable'. It was not long before weekly or evening papers in many parts of the country were bringing out their own results editions, often merely adding a results page to the final issue of the ordinary paper. The first sports-only Saturday special was probably the one produced by Tillotsons of Bolton, the *Football Field and Sports Telegram*, from 1884. Nothing could beat the evening paper in the race to be first with the news, and, more importantly, the winners and the scores. Nor was it only local or national sports news which was featured. Well before 1914, evening papers from Plymouth to Newcastle could include the full scorecard plus a 150-word description of the play in the Australia–England cricket test in Sydney, supplied by the Press Association for ten shillings a day including the cost of the telegrams.

Early sports writers tended to be well-educated gentlemen, their prose distributed in long columns, liberally punctuated by classical allusions and quotations. By the interwar years such writers had all but disappeared save from the very best papers. The popular press went for bigger headlines, eye-catching pictures and a more capricious approach. The writers themselves began to be drawn from the lower middle class and working classes. After the Second World War the competition in Fleet Street prompted a lust for sensations in sport, as in other walks of life. Far from keeping their distance from the sportsman, so that familiarity might not impair judgement, the aim was to get closer, so that the inside stories would be uncovered. No longer need they be about sport itself. Indeed the private lives of the sportsmen and sports-women increasingly made much better copy. The language of the sports page was progressively characterized by chauvi-nism, aggression and studied bad taste.

It was the press who first elevated a minority of sportsmen and women into national celebrities, whose names and faces were recognized even by people uninterested in sport; per-formers whose mere presence on the pitch, at the wicket, on the court or the track would tempt people to the event; the exceptional performer who set the standards of achievement for the majority of more or less ordinary players. Tom Sayers, the mid-Victorian prize fighter was probably the first such star and W. G. Grace undoubtedly the second, becoming the most famous Victorian, ahead even of Gladstone. His image decorated not only newspapers and magazines, but cigarette cards and porcelain. Cricket as the national game has rarely been short of national heroes but none of them, from the Indian Prince Ranjitsinhji to Jack Hobbs and Len Hutton would equal the long lived magnetism of W. G. If he had not died during the First World War there would probably have been a national day of mourning. In the 1930s Fred Perry was probably all that most people knew of tennis, Joe Davis performed the same role for snooker and Henry Cotton for golf. Horse-racing captivated people at both ends of the social spectrum and successful jockeys attracted not only the punters and their money but celebrity status. Steve Donoghue in the 1920s and Gordon Richards from the 1930s to the 1950s were the Lester Piggotts of their time. It is no accident that it was Hobbs, the cricketer, and Richards, the jockey, who were the first sportsmen to be knighted. The people's game was full of heroes, but national celebrity status in that sport had to await radio and TV coverage after 1945, together with an expanding middle-class interest that accompanied it. Billy Meredith played until he was fifty and was perhaps the first star player. But Stanley Matthews was the first to achieve the kind of national recognition reached by the other sportsmen mentioned here. He was also the first footballer to receive a public honour – interestingly only a CBE in 1957. His knighthood came later.

Newspaper coverage of sport contributed to its extension and growth, not merely by providing publicity and advertising but by identifying it as an important part of British culture. In return, sporting news sold papers, or at least owners and editors thought it did. In effect the development of sport benefited from newspaper coverage even more surely than it put money into the pockets of the press lords. There did not seem any way in which the press could do sport permanent damage except by ignoring it.

But radio was a different matter. Newspapers could preview an event or they could describe it after it had taken place. Radio could tell the listener what was happening while it was happening. That might certainly be a threat to the generally cosy relationship which sport and newspapers had constructed by the 1920s: it might also undermine one of the main attractions of the newspaper itself. The Newspaper Proprietors' Association made known its anxieties as early as 1923, complaining that the 'broadcasting of racing and football results and similar matter would certainly seriously interfere with the sale of newspapers'. Three years later the NPA included racing and betting news along with birth control in a list of dangerous subjects which, if broadcast, 'would be highly objectionable to a large section of the community'. But what was already a bad wicket for the newspaper owners became decidedly sticky once the BBC ceased to be a private company and became a public corporation. As such it could hardly be denied access to so important a cultural sector as sport. In 1927 the BBC began broadcasting commentaries on live sporting events and that year the England–Wales Rugby Union International, an FA cup-tie, the Grand National, the Oxford and Cambridge athletics match, the Boat Race, the Amateur Golf Championship and Wimbledon were all covered. By 1934 the first full afternoons of broadcast sport were being transmitted with the scene shifting back and forth between a whole galaxy of sports some less popular than others. Even then the newspaper proprietors were able to exert some pressure. It was not until after the Second World War that the Saturday afternoon football results could be broadcast before 6 p.m. The evening papers maintained, until then, their exclusive position of being first with the news.

It was not only the newspaper owners who were supicious of the new medium and determined to protect their interests. Not all sports were keen to be broadcast. The Football League, for example, was convinced that live commentaries even on the second half of matches would affect attendances and for several years refused to allow them. This gave the adventurous young men at the BBC the opportunity to exercise their ingenuity. 'The Football Association [*sic*] remained obstinate about letting us broadcast on League matches but I can remember our trying to circumvent their decision by sending in relays of eye-witnesses who paid their entrance money in the ordinary way and came out in sequence to broadcast about the part of the match that they had seen.'[1] The problem was to recur, in a very different socio-economic context and with more serious consequences for football, with the growth of television. In general, the less popular the sport, the keener it was to take advantage of the BBC's power to reach almost every home in the land.

In the interwar years BBC radio was dominated by the notions of its Director-General, John Reith. No aspect of the Corporation's output escaped the improving and educational ideals he sought to foster. Sport was not there merely to be described: it was also to be understood and it was important that it promoted the correct social attitudes. Some sporting programmes clearly had these goals in mind, like the one in September 1932 in which a referee gave a talk entitled 'Association Football, the Referee and the Spectator', stressing the importance of all players accepting the referee's decision as final. The special place of cricket in British sporting life was reflected by the BBC North Region Executive taking out memberships of both Lancashire and Yorkshire County Cricket Clubs in 1936. Sport was not to be exempt from 'BBC Standards'. That meant that the starting prices of the first three past the post were not part of the racing results until long after the Second World War. It also meant, for example, that even in 1948, the policy of the Home Service was to reflect 'the reputable sports world which meant golf, rowing, lawn tennis, and something called "rugger".' The stress was to be on amateur sport and on people playing games rather than watching them: 'humble endeavour maybe, but good sportsmanship and no transfer fee'.[2]

Radio certainly helped to consolidate the position, already attained by some sporting events, as key moments in a national sporting calendar. The Boat Race, the Cup Final, the Derby, test matches and Wimbledon were the highlights of the radio sporting year as they were to become the highlights of BBC television's sporting year after 1945. Commentators gradually improved after trial and error and demonstrated the superiority of the microphone expert over the subject

[53]

expert, and the coming of the car radio and the transistor helped to ensure that sport on radio kept a sizeable audience even in the television age. For one thing TV cannot always obtain live coverage. Moreover some football fans, for example, want to know what is going on at other grounds. One of the earliest examples of a supporter taking what must have been a fairly cumbersome, battery-powered radio to a match in order to listen to the sound commentary from another game was reported from Stoke in 1928.

By the 1960s watching television was the principal leisure activity for most people in Britain, cutting across all ages and classes. Sport was bound to be attractive to such a medium if for no other reason than it was cheap and already popular. For the audience, watching an event on television was infinitely preferable to having it described by a radio commentator. Even the highlights, shown after the event, were an advance on the live radio broadcast. 'Watching the sport' was often given as the main reason for buying a TV set in the late 1950s and early 1960s; and the week before the Cup Final was a time when both retailers and rental companies did particularly good business.

Technical improvements naturally served to enhance the attractiveness of sport on television. Outside broadcast teams, including not only cameramen but engineers and riggers, had the benefit of the roving eye camera from 1955. Pictures could be shown while the camera was on the move. Events could be covered at short notice. And no longer were these events confined to these islands. The opening of the Euro-vision Link precipitated fifty-eight hours of live coverage of the Rome Olympics in 1960. From 1968 the introduction of colour made sport seem even more realistic and spectacular. As Garry Whannel has pointed out, television coverage is now so sophisticated that a 'seamless blend' of live action, recorded highlights, action replays, interviews, previews and postscripts can be presented to the viewer such that it is no longer possible to describe TV as relaying an event: 'rather it is producing an elaborate, entertaining show, based upon the event'.

Television, of course, became the pre-eminent maker of

national sporting celebrities, elevating to star status any sportsmen or women, provided they could offer success and especially if some panache or personality went with it. Footballers and ice skaters, cricketers and snooker players, athletes, boxers, rugby players and even horses have been, and will continue to be, raised to the sporting purple over-night. The Birthday and New Year's Honours now have a regular sporting spot – a recognition of a national status that media and audience have already conferred. The sports star contributes to society's myth of success. Anyone can do it with talent, some luck and, of course, the professionalism of hard work. And the appeal of the champion who cannot be beaten remains powerful.

In 1977, the annual report on the future of broadcasting claimed the coverage of sport on television and radio as 'one of the success stories of broadcasting'. But this scarcely stands up to close scrutiny. There must be some doubt as to whether television coverage of sport adequately reflects the real popularity of particular sports. Angling and squash, for example, are clearly mass-participation sports but neither feature very often in television sports programmes. Angling perhaps does not have the right rhythms nor frequent enough action to suit the cameras and the technical diffi-culties of showing two competitors pursuing a small, fast-moving, black ball in a confined space have never been overcome. Television coverage did much to boost the popu-larity of show-jumping, swimming and gymnastics, yet dur-ing the winter of 1985–6 it failed to offer any significant coverage of the West Indies–England cricket matches. In 1981 twelve sports cornered 85 per cent of all television sports coverage. It is a matter for discussion whether tele-vision should spread that cover over a greater number of sports.

As for the coverage that is offered, it is clear that some sports suit the small rectangular screen very well. Boxing, tennis and snooker can not only be shown complete, as it were, but the expressions on the faces of the participants can be clearly seen and add to the drama of those events. Football is not presented so easily. It is a game where rapid movement off the ball is of the essence, but cannot be shown because no camera has a sufficiently wide angle of vision to cover enough of the field.

A second criticism that might be made of television coverage of sport is that it too readily succumbs to the pressure to make it all 'entertaining'. This is partly the result of the competition for audience ratings between BBC and ITV. Both sides know that the sports enthusiast will watch anyway. The 'entertainment' for him, or her, comes from the unpredictability of the outcome and the partisanship involved. Most people want one side or one player to win and a good deal of the excitement provoked by sport is the result of these fancies. But it is the even larger numbers beyond those already hooked that television is out to recruit. Exciting football matches, fights in the ring, even snooker, cannot be guaranteed. Neither can record times and heights. So the packaged programme, with the highlights from previous matches, pregame discussions, slow-motion replays, the whole gamut of technical expertise that is now at the programme makers' disposal, is used to prevent the fringe audience from turning off or, what is much worse, turning to the other channel. Sport is not part of the entertainment industry in the way that television is. But television is continually tempted to treat it as if it were. One of the most irritating ways it does this is by fudging the demarcation line between the two by showing, for example, pro-am celebrity golf or snooker matches. As Benny Green once said, no one cares about the TV rights for the northern area bantamweight championship but if Morecambe and Wise fought for it the promoters would be trampled in the rush.

The obsession with sport as *entertainment* leads to the more serious charge that the educational role, which we saw earlier was a central feature of BBC radio's sporting coverage during the Reith era and after, is now being neglected. That the ideal has not completely disappeared is shown by looking again at the Annan Report. 'What they [BBC and ITV] can do, as well as entertain, is increase people's understanding of a game's basic principles, refine the appreciation of armchair experts and inspire some to take an active part in sport themselves.' But it is difficult to be educative without being critical and criticism is made more than awkward if the relationship between the sport and the medium is too close. The continued employment of football managers on panels; the inevitable interview with the winner, even occasionally the loser, in which no attempt is made to ask more than the conventional unprobing questions met usually by the inarticulate or defensive clichéd answer; the anxiety shown by the sports departments of both major television and radio organizations to be on close terms with the players and administrators: all these factors create a huge obstacle to what ought to be one of the medium's tasks. In 1945 BBC radio's sports committee discussed the idea that the Corporation should fairly reflect all recognized sport 'but must allow itself an editorial view'. It must keep on good terms with the world of sports promotion 'but never at the cost of bad reporting'. Is this policy being followed when professional boxing promoters are accredited officially as BBC reporters for the amateur tournament at the Commonwealth Games, and when football managers are regularly allowed to point out to Jimmy Hill – himself, for a time, managing director of a football club – that emphasizing the negative aspects 'of the game will bring it into disrepute and should be stopped'? It is not merely the task of the sports departments at BBC and ITV to celebrate sporting achievement: it should also be their job to treat sport with the same degree of inquisitiveness that they would apply to the National Health Service or the British aerospace industry. Unfortunately they demonstrate all too clearly that sport is too serious a matter to be left to television and radio sports programmers.

Finally there is the question of whether international sport on British television is presented with unacceptable chauvinism. It is clear that the BBC have always been worried about this. Commentators during the 1940s and 1950s were regularly warned not to take sides. In 1949, for example, commentators were told before the England v. Italy football match 'to build partisanship in the viewer' while not groaning whenever an English movement broke down. Again there was some suggestion that too much bias had been shown by radio commentators during matches between English and Hungarian sides in the 1950s. Sound commentators were given a list of things to avoid in 1955. One of them was taking sides. The others were 'do not be tentative; do not exaggerate and do not make mistakes'. It is probably inevitable that the national interest in any sporting event will be the first priority. Sport and partisanship cannot be totally divorced, nor should they be. It is how Britishness is defined and the danger of slipping into the stereotypical cliché which has to be guarded against. After the World Cup of 1986, it is difficult to avoid the feeling that televised football is the worst offender.

Sport has to be strong to stand up to television. In the United States, television is so powerful it can compel the rescheduling of matches in the National Tennis Championships to suit its own programming and make the Baseball World Series take place on cool October evenings. The two World Cups in Mexico played all the matches in the heat of the day in order to satisfy the demands of European television. It can be a ruthless taskmaster. In Britain the national winter game, football, a game in crisis, lacking leadership, suffering falling support and unable to match its playing standards with the best, fought a battle with television in 1983, largely over money, and lost. It seems strange, especially given the American example, that when live matches are televised they are not blacked out in the immediate vicinity of the ground. As this is not done, crowds are smaller than they would otherwise be. The suggestion is often made that television also changes people's attitudes to sport. By bringing the best into their homes, it makes them impatient with anything less. It is difficult to believe that many more people would go to Doncaster Rovers or Doncaster Rugby League Club if sport was suddenly removed from their television screens. As it is, such a consummation is most unlikely to take place, however devoutly wished for by that section of the population who do not find sport very interesting. In the summer of 1986, for example, BBC television's total budget was about £50 million, of which between £15 million and £20 million was spent on sport. The really big sporting events can capture very large audiences. The 1986 World Cup Final was watched in Britain by 22.5 million people, 9 million saw the men's single final at Wimbledon and 11 million the final night of the World Snooker Championship. Moreover, such events can often attract large audiences at times when most people are in bed. So the relationship between sport and television will remain close. The question is whether sport can ever attain a position of strength from which to negotiate or whether the merry-go-round identified by John Arlott in the *Guardian* of 17 November 1982 will continue indefinitely.

> The governing bodies of sport want to see an image presented which does full or overfull justice to the sport, and money. The players want good publicity, to win, and money. The viewer wants entertainment and the broadcaster an unbroken series of highlights.

### 3 Gambling and sport

Gambling has always been a part of the modern sporting world, although the public response to it has varied from one period to another. Gambling was endemic in eighteenth-century Britain, but before 1850 a puritanical reaction had begun, aimed particularly at working-class betting. The greatest achievement of the anti-gambling lobby was probably the Street Betting Act of 1906, but it remained a powerful and influential opponent certainly up until the second Royal Commission on the subject in 1949. Since then gambling on sport has been increasingly raided by governments to provide income for the state and has also played a crucial role in the financing of the major sports of football and horse-racing.

Betting had always been a part of rural sports, both those involving animals, such as cock-fighting and bear-baiting, and those involving contests between men. Pedestrianism, for example, probably began in the seventeenth and eighteenth centuries, when aristocrats and gentry promoted races between their footmen. These men had been used as message carriers between town house and country residence,

[59]

although this function lapsed as roads improved and coaches became speedier and more reliable. Their masters often gambled heavily on the results of such races. Sometimes the young master ran himself. Pedestrianism, like prize fighting, seems to have enjoyed a fashionable period from about 1790–1810. It could almost be characterized as the jogging of the early nineteenth century. Its most famous gentlemanly practitioner was Captain Barclay, a Scottish landowner whose real name was Robert Barclay Allardice. He was prepared to bet a thousand guineas in 1801 that he would walk ninety miles in twenty-one and a half hours. He failed twice and lost his money each time. But on 10 November 1801 he did it, for a stake of 5,000 guineas.

Betting on horses was also commonplace, often taking the form of individual challenges between members of the landed classes. In the eighteenth century it was the usual practice to ride your own horse, but the employment of a professional jockey became increasingly common. Betting added another dimension of excitement to the uncertainty of sport itself and it was excitement which the leisured rural classes were especially seeking, particularly in a countryside whose range of more conventional pursuits soon began to pall in the eyes of the young, married, leisured, pleasure-seeking males.

Cricket was another rural pastime that the landed bucks found attractive. By the beginning of the eighteenth century newspaper advertisements told of forthcoming matches 'between eleven gentlemen of a west part of the county of Kent, against as many of Chatham, for eleven guineas a man'. With money at stake it was important to reduce the chances of disagreement by drawing up a body of rules and regulations by which both sides would abide. In this way gambling made its contribution to the development of the laws of cricket. In fact, in the code of 1774 it was specifically mentioned:

> If the notches of one player are laid against another, the Bet depends on both Innings, unless otherwise specified.
> If one Party beats the other in one Innings, the Notches in

the first Innings shall determine the Bet.
But if the other Party goes in a Second Time then the Bet must be determined by the numbers on the score.

Football was, of course, a very attractive proposition both to bookmakers and punters. Before 1900 some newspapers had offered prizes for forecasting the correct scores as well as the results of a small number of matches and early in the twentieth century a system of betting on football coupons at fixed odds had developed in the North of England. It has been suggested that the early pools might have been partly emulating the pigeon pools by which a prize fund was collected for a particular pigeon race, with each competitor subscribing. The owner of the winning bird collected.

Newspapers began publishing their own pools coupons (until the Courts declared the practice illegal in 1928) and individual bookmakers offered a variety of betting opportunities. By the end of the 1920s, the football pools, and particularly Littlewoods, under the entrepreneurial guidance of the Moores brothers, had begun to thrive. The pool for one week in 1929–30 reached £19,000. By the mid-1930s the firm was sponsoring programmes on Radio Luxembourg which broadcast the results of matches on Saturdays and Sundays. The football coupon asked backers to forecast the results of a given number of matches from a long list or a selected short list. The latter was given attractive names like 'family four' and 'easy six', three draws or four aways. In January 1935 the penny points was introduced and soon became the favourite pool with the largest dividends, consisting of fourteen matches chosen for their special degree of difficulty. The eight-draw treble chance replaced it as the most popular pool after 1945. By 1935 estimates put the number of punters at between five and seven million and it was ten million by the time war broke out. In 1934 those companies founding the Pools Promoters' Association had a turnover of about £8 million which had increased by 1938 to £22 million of which the promoters retained a little over 20 per cent. This is not the place to animadvert on the place of the pools in British society.

By the mid-nineteenth century, therefore, betting and sport were firmly established as the closest of associates. But the middle-class evangelicalism of the new urban industrial Britain was already beginning to take steps against what was increasingly characterized as a social evil. Gambling was typical of a corrupt aristocracy and it served them right if it led to the sale of their estates and the impoverishment of ancient families. But when the poor were led to emulate those who should have set a better example then something had to be done. By 1850 the state was being pressurized into doing it. The arguments used by the opponents of working-class betting remained more or less unchanged for the next one hundred years. Betting by the poor led to debt which led to crime. Even where crime was avoided, deterioration of character was not, especially among the young and women. Spending sums on betting which could not be afforded weakened the material basis of family life thereby making a major contribution to poverty. Finally gambling undermined proper attitudes to work. As *The Times* so succinctly put it in the 1890s, it 'eats the heart out of honest labour. It produces an impression that life is governed by chance and not by laws.' These arguments carried most days until the Royal Commission of 1949–51.

The anti-gamblers' first legislative success was an Act of 1853 to suppress betting houses and betting shops which had been springing up in many places, very often inside public houses. In future, bookmakers operating from such places, exhibiting lists or in any way informing the public that they were prepared to take bets were liable to a fine of £100 and a six-month prison sentence. The Bill went through both Houses without a debate. Betting shops may have found difficulty in surviving: betting itself moved outside, to the streets and places of employment. The expansion of horse-racing in particular, with, after 1870, the electric telegraph and a cheap press providing tips and results, provoked the opposition to organize itself, which eventually resulted in the formation of the National Anti-Gambling League. It was in its heyday in the two decades or so before 1914. Sociologists such as B. S. Rowntree, the economist J. A. Hobson and radical politicans like J. Ramsay MacDonald contributed to its publications. They saw the working-class gambler exploited by the bookmaker and those upper-class sportmen who supported him. After failing with the law the League turned to Parliament with the clear aim of eradicating street betting. It was this off-course variety which was responsible for the bulk of working-class gambling. A House of Lords Select Committee first examined the matter in 1901–2. In 1906 came the legislation.

The Street Betting Act of 1906 has gained some notoriety as an example of class biased legislation. It was not aimed at all off-course betting. A person who could afford an account with a bookmaker who knew his financial circumstances well enough to allow him to bet on credit did not have a problem. This ruled out many working men and women. It was ready-money betting of the sort they went in for that was to be prosecuted. In future it was to be an offence for any person to frequent or loiter in a street or public place on behalf of himself or any other person for the purpose of bookmaking or betting or wagering or agreeing to bet or wager or paying or receiving or settling bets.

It is unlikely that the Act did much to diminish the amount of betting. It did, of course, enhance the excitement of it all, especially at those times and in those places where local magistrates decided that the full rigour of the law must be enforced. Moreover it placed the police in an increasingly difficult position trying to enforce a law for which there was little popular support. Allegations that they frequently looked the other way or had an agreement with local bookmakers to prosecute a runner from each of them in turn were commonplace. By 1929 the police were very critical of both the law and their role in enforcing it and said so before the Royal Commission which was examining the police service in that year. It took the liberalizing impact of the Second World War and the relatively buoyant economic circumstances which eventually succeeded it to bring about a more relaxed attitude to gambling. This was also facilitated by the Royal Commission of 1949–51 having relatively sophisticated economic and statistical apparatus which enabled it to show that personal expenditure on gambling was only about 1 per cent of total personal expenditure, that gambling was then absorbing only about 0.5 per cent of the total resources of the country and that it was by then rare for it to be a cause of poverty in individual households. They still regarded gambling as a fairly low-level activity and were not impressed by the amount of intellectual effort some enthusiasts brought to it. But they were in favour of the provision of legal facilities for betting off the course and the licensed betting shop reappeared in 1960, 107 years after it had first been made illegal. Six years later the Government's betting duty reappeared too.

Gambling's relationship with sport has been significant in two other respects: as a motive for malpractice and corruption and as a source of finance for sporting activities. The latter is closely connected to the growth of football pools of which more in a moment. Not all sports lend themselves to result fixing with equal facility. The team games should, in theory, prove the most difficult, because there are so many more players who would have to be 'squared' if an agreed result was to be secured. In the early nineteenth century the relatively small number of professionals could exert a disproportionate influence on some cricket matches and they were occasionally bribed or removed from the game by false reports of sickness in the family. One professional was banned from Lord's in 1817 for allegedly 'selling' the match between England and Nottingham. The gradual assumption of authority by the MCC and the county clubs, the improvement in the material rewards of the average professional cricketer and the increasing opportunities to bet on other sports – notably horse-racing and, after 1926, greyhound racing – probably killed off gambling on cricket by cricketers. Today the Test and County Cricket Board (TCCB) has a regulation forbidding players to gamble on matches in which they take part. It was thought to be overly cynical even by late twentieth-century standards when Dennis Lillee and Rodney Marsh won £5,000 and £2,500 respectively by betting against their own team, Australia, in the Leeds Test of 1981. By then, of course, betting by spectators could be encouraged because it brought in revenue. Ladbrokes had been allowed to pitch their tent at Lord's since 1973.

Football has occasionally been shaken by allegations that matches have been thrown, usually in the context of championship, promotion or relegation struggles. Attempts to fix the results of matches in order to bring off betting coups appear to have been very rare but in 1964 ten players received prison sentences for their part in a so-called betting ring. Three of the players were prominent English internationals and they were banned from football playing and management for life. Two, Peter Swan and David Layne, were later reinstated on appeal but by then were too old to take up where they had left off. Certainly the FA and the Football League were anxious to keep betting and football apart. When coupon betting first appeared in the North of England, before 1914, the FA Council threatened to suspend permanently any player or official who could be proved to have taken part in it. In 1913 they failed, but in 1920 succeeded in getting Parliament to push through a bill forbidding ready-money betting on football matches.

Football itself had not profited from the growth of pools. But it seems clear that early in 1935 discussions were taking place between the League's Management Committee and representatives of the Pools Promoters' Association about the possibility of the pools making a payment to the League for the use of their fixtures. But the public attitude of many of the leaders of League football was that the pools constituted a menace to the game and should be suppressed either by the action of the football authorities or by state intervention via an Act of Parliament. The negotiations broke down, perhaps because the pools promoters did not wish to pay what was being asked so long as there was some doubt about whether the fixtures were copyright. All out war was declared and an attempt made to damage the pools by secretly changing the fixtures on two consecutive Saturdays at the end of February and the beginning of March 1936. Unfortunately for the Football League, dissension in the ranks led to the plans being leaked and the scheme sank. They had no better luck with a private members bill to abolish the pools which was easily defeated in the Commons in the same year. Moreover, the League felt it did not need tainted money from the pools, whose promoters therefore kept their hands in their pockets. They did not take them out again until 1959 (although they offered to, briefly, at the end of the war).

It is hard to escape the feeling that not only football but sport in Britain missed a real financial opportunity, although it is clear that it would have required government help to have realized it. In the 1930s the private firms running British football pools set up offices and agencies in several European countries. In Sweden, for example, where betting on pools was illegal, around 200,000 people were completing coupons every week, the stake money swelling the profits of Littlewoods and Vernons among others. The Swedish Government acted to stop it in 1934 by establishing the Swedish Betting Corporation to run a state owned pool. Switzerland and Finland soon followed and, by 1950, similar state-run pools had begun in Norway, Spain, Italy, West Germany, Denmark and Austria. Later Poland, Czechoslovakia, Belgium and Holland adopted similar schemes. After administration and prize money had been found, much of what remained was channelled into the support not merely of football but of sport and physical recreation in general. For example £8 million had been so raised by the Swedish Government over a three-year period at the end of the 1930s. There were three moments when a similar scheme might have been set up in this country.

The first was early in the Second World War when it was clear that some rationalization of existing commercial institutions in a range of fields would have to take place. The Secretary of the Football Association, Stanley Rous, together with Sir Arthur Elvin, who ran Wembley Stadium, proposed the creation of an independent pools company, half of whose profits would go to football. Nothing came of it. Instead the government agreed to an amalgamation of the existing companies for the duration. It was known as Unity Pools.

Rous returned to the problem with even more radical proposals in 1943. Reconstruction was in the air and he had been finding out about Sweden in particular. Rous proposed that appropriate Government departments should be approached with the suggestion that part of the proceeds from the pools should go into a centrally administered fund, out of which would come money for sports grounds, gymnasia, recreation rooms and sports centres. Again nothing came of it.

The subject was raised for a third time during the sitting of the Royal Commission on Betting Lotteries and Gaming, 1949–51. The English, Scottish and Welsh Football Associations all supported the idea of a non-profit-making football pool under Government control. But the Commission disagreed, partly because they felt a considerable body of public opinion would not like it, partly because of practical difficulties and partly because of the loss of revenue to the Government. If there had been a moment for such radical change, it must have been during those reforming years of the third Labour Government. By 1951, its legs were very shaky indeed. Moreover it had been the Labour Government that had instituted a 10 per cent tax on the pools in 1947 and increased it to 30 per cent in 1949. Football, of course, could always do its own deal with the pools and in the summer of 1959 it did. In the previous October the Football League had issued a writ against Littlewoods claiming that the League fixtures for the following season were its copyright. In May 1959 a judge agreed. By July an agreement had been signed, to last for ten years, by which the Pools Promoters' Association was to pay the Football League and the Scottish League a royalty of 0.5 per cent on total stake money, which would not be less than £245,000 a year. There have been several subsequent agreements, the latest a twelve-year one signed in December 1984 which ensures the Football League £5 million per year. This, though, is but a small proportion of the income of the pools companies, three of whom – Littlewoods, Vernons and Zetters – paid the Government £220 million in tax in 1984–5 but still made a profit of £17 million.[3]

The treatment of football was different to that of horse-racing. The Government did not introduce a tax on gambling on horse-racing until 1966. In 1985 it was still being levied at only 8 per cent. As we saw above, the tax on pools betting came much earlier and was much higher: 42 per cent in 1985. When betting shops were legalized the Government established a Horserace Betting Levy Board, allegedly to compensate racecourses for the fall in attendance that would ensue. Its role was to assess and collect a levy from bookmakers and the tote and use the money for the benefit of racing. According to the leading authority on the subject, the Levy Board saved racing in this country. Perhaps there should be a Football Betting Levy Board. It is not clear why there has not been. British sport has had to get on terms with gambling in the twentieth century; it seems that the terms could have been better.

# 3
# Theory and opinion

Twenty-five years ago it would not have been too great a departure from the truth to claim that those people interested in sport and those interested in social and political theory were, on the whole, not the same people. Serious thinkers tended to ignore sport. This is not so today. The sociology of sport, for example, has become a vigorous sub-discipline in universities and colleges – particularly in the United States – and throughout the world. Academic journals devoted to sport are numerous, including one on the *Philosophy of Sport*. In Britain one of the foremost socialist political theorists of the age, Ralph Miliband, has offered the opinion that 'sport culture deserves, from the point of view of the making and the un-making of class consciousness, much more attention than it has received ... The elaboration of a Marxist sociology of sport may not be the most urgent of theoretical tasks; but it is not the most negligible of tasks either'. It is a task already in progress.

Organized sport first came to prominence on a large scale in late nineteenth-century Britain and America and it was from the United States that one of the most distinguished early attempts to explain sport's social importance came. In 1899 the American sociologist Thorsten Veblen published his classic work, *The Theory of the Leisure Class*. It was based on a study of America's contemporary ruling élite and sport was identified as a prominent feature of élite life. Sport afforded 'an exercise for dexterity and for the emulative ferocity and astuteness characteristic of predatory life . . . So long as the individual is but slightly gifted with reflection or with a sense of the ulterior trend of his actions – so long as his life is substantially a life of naive, impulsive action – so long as the immediate and unreflected purposefulness of sports, in the way of an expression of dominance, will measurably satisfy his instinct of workmanship'. Sport was therefore attractive to the leisured classes, because it was both exclusive and futile. It was also, according to Veblen, a sign of the 'arrested development' of man's moral nature. He likened the relationship of football to physical culture as that of the bullfight to agriculture. Of course, he had American football in mind, a game which at the time he wrote was not only mainly for college students but was an activity of such coarseness and brutality that the President of the United States intervened to precipitate both rule changes and the wearing of protective clothing in order to cut down the number of deaths – there had been eighteen in the autumn of 1905 alone. (It is worth pointing out that there were 71 deaths and 366 serious injuries in Yorkshire Rugby between 1890 and 1893.) J. A. Hobson, a British admirer of Veblen, extended his idea of sport as the essence of the predatory instinct by equating jingoism and British Imperialism with the 'lust of the spectator'. Applauding militarism and watching professional athletes stemmed from the same perverted appetites.

Neither Veblen nor Hobson liked sport and they particularly disliked the mass spectacle that they thought it was increasingly becoming. Many British socialists, both before and after the Great War, shared that mistrust and anxiety. Participation in games or physical exercise designed to improve the health of the body was one thing: it was quite another to watch paid athletes perform in circumstances which could hardly fail to remind the observer of the gladiatorial contests of the ancient world, deliberately aimed to distract an exploited labour force. Even amateur sport seemed infected by the virus of the competitive élites. Here

was yet another case of the unhealthy dissemination down-
wards of values which appeared the opposite of co-operative,
caring and democratic. Sport was part of the dominant
culture. How could it serve the cause of socialism? How could
you be a socialist and go to football matches?

Of course Fascism in Italy, via the leisure organization the
Dopolavoro, and in Nazi Germany increasingly glorified sport
and the physical conditioning of the body as the essential
preparation for a nation in arms. Veblen's idea that the
ferocity and cunning associated with sport were only useful
in hostile dealings with other communities seemed to have
become real. Even in sport-loving Britain, Oswald Mosley
claimed that the statesman should be like the athlete who has
trained himself to the peak at the right moment.

However, there had been a lively workers' sports movement in Europe, notably in Germany and Austria, before the
First World War. Its aim was to attract young workers to
participate in healthy and enjoyable play and physical activities in a socialist atmosphere. The movement favoured equal-
ity of opportunity and opposed the élitism and what it
thought of as the competitive obsessions of bourgeois or
capitalist sports. But relations within the German Social
Democratic Party, for example, between the sports enthusiasts and the rest were never easy. A certain contempt on the
one side was matched by a little anti-intellectualism on the
other. Moreover, although the movement had tended to
favour the less competitive activities such as cycling, gymnastics, hiking and swimming, its members, after 1918, found
themselves pushed into embracing the more popular team
games like football and track and field athletics. In Britain,
where bourgeois sport was most highly developed, there was
no similar organization until the British Workers' Sports
Federation of the 1920s. This was, in fact, a Communist Party
front organization and, in 1930, the Labourist National
Workers' Sports Association was set up to oppose it, thus
completing in Britain the institutional political split which
was by then a feature of the European workers' sports
movement between the Communist Red Sports International
and the Social Democratic Sports group.

This must have been a bitter disappointment for activitists in the European workers' sports movement who had doubt-less hoped that the new Soviet Socialist Republic would inaugurate a new era of people's sport to match the changes elsewhere in the new society. In fact, and in summary, the new regime's attitude to sport went through three phases. The first, immediately following the Revolution itself, was characterized by a concentration on sport only in so far as it contributed to the development of a physically fit population. The second phase during the later 1920s comprised hostility to the competitive sports of the capitalists with an underlying commitment to sport as a contributor to the people's health. Finally, in the 1930s, the Stalinist cult of performance was introduced. John Hoberman in his book, *Sport and Political Ideology*, summed up this phase succinctly. 'The Stalinist athlete may be seen as a sporting analogue to the Stakhano-vite worker of the mid-1930s, the heroic record-breaker who vastly over-fulfilled the production quota to build socialism.'

Since the Soviet Union competed in the Olympic Games for the first time in 1952 the continuing competitive nature of sport in the socialist world has seemed to bear striking similarities to sport in the West. Some Marxists have not found any difficulty with this situation. For them, sport in the Eastern Bloc reflects the humanistic world view of commu-nist culture. Practically it plays a part in increasing economic productivity, contributes to military defence and, at interna-tional contests and sports meetings, the success of Eastern European athletes demonstrates to the world, if not the superiority of Communism as ideology or regime, at least that it can compete on equal terms with the sports-obsessed West.

The 1960s, culminating in the radical movements in Paris and West Germany in 1968, stimulated a more critical Marxist or, as it is often termed, neo-Marxist structuralist critique of sport in both West and East. As it is in tune with the criticisms of sport offered by mainstream functionalism and is typical of more general criticisms of sport's role in modern society it seems appropriate to examine here the major points of that critique. The examination will focus particularly on the work of a leading protagonist, Bero Rigauer.

Rigauer's book, *Sport und Arbeit*, was first published in Frankfurt in 1970 and did not appear in English until 1981 when the leading sports historian of the United States, Allen Guttmann, both introduced and translated it. The aim of the book was certainly ambitious. It was to produce a comprehensive critical theory of contemporary sport. Not only that, but the hope was clearly expressed that this was a book not simply concerned to analyse society but to play its part in changing it. The starting point of the critique was that sport and work were structurally analogous. Far from modern sport being the opposite of work, at the highest level it shared the main features of industrial production: discipline, authority, competition, achievement, rationalization and bureaucracy. The bourgeois élite in late-nineteenth-century Britain would have been shocked by these claims. For them, sport was different from work: a relief from it, an area of life – like the home and family – where different values should flourish. Also, contrary to Rigauer's theory, sport was a subject of debate, not simply between classes, but within them too. It was in such a context that disagreement arose around questions and definitions of amateurism and professionalism, participation as against spectatorism and around the whole idea of whether sport was making a positive contribution to British society. Rigauer has little patience with such niceties. For him, the middle-class élite wanted to persuade the exploited that sport was different from work, only in order to deceive. Sport could then function as an aid to production by improving the health of the young and not-so-young worker and thus reduce the time lost at work through illness. It could also aid the growth of militarism and nationalism. Or it could indeed function as an illusory island of freedom in a world which saw the vast majority struggling in a Sargasso Sea of ill-rewarded labour.

For Rigauer, the adverse consequences of all this for sport are very clear. In the first place, in such a context, competition and even interpersonal relations in sport became 'prone to antagonistic forms'. Increasingly the emphasis becomes quantitative and abstract. What is important is what can be measured. The top-level athlete's freedom and creativity is limited because the performances in which he takes part are run and organized by someone else with goals, of profit making for example, which are not necessarily those which the athlete or sportsman would have freely chosen. Top-level sport becomes dominated by money. In football, for example, the so-called players are themselves reduced to commodities and are often bought and sold in a world market-place. The result is a dehumanization which is exacerbated by labelling any diminution in the athlete's capacity to perform as failure.

Sporting performances at the top level are, Rigauer would claim, over-rationalized and planned, being carefully calculated and worked out in advance because of the adherence to the achievement principle and the need to succeed. This means, *inter alia*, that training becomes as subdivided as the division of labour in industry. Sportsmen and women spend more time in training than actually competing. They will almost certainly find that decisions about how they train, what they eat, how they live even, will be made by those placed in authority over them. Sport is run by a whole series of bureaucracies with little if any operational democracy. Science is used in a very questionable way to ensure that the athlete goes faster, farther or higher, or stays on the field even when his physical state demands that he should come off it. This is as true of Eastern Europe as the West. What is clear, Rigauer claims, is that any playfulness or spontaneity which may have been part of top-level sport is lost.

His conclusions are therefore unambiguously grim. Sport and work, far from being at opposite ends of the spectrum of human activity, are reflections of the same perverted vision. The emphasis on regular performance and achievement demands that for the top-level sportsman sport becomes work. If it does not he will soon be eliminated from the sporting élite. Even the language used by participants to describe what they do and how they do it is littered with references to hard work and work rate. Top-level athletes work at sport, often taking years of hard work to reach the top. Finally, sport is reactionary. The qualities valued in top-level sport – ambition, conscientiousness, drive, recognition of hierarchy and authority – are conservative and conformist.

Rigauer offers no detailed prescription for improving the health of sport. But he does suggest that under a socialist mode of production, sport and work might come together in a symbolic unity. Sport would, of course, be democratized, and its essentially political nature recognized. In short, the reality of the connections between sport and society would not be at best played down or at worst denied, as they so often are now, but unambiguously illuminated by a critical theory that would demystify sport as it would all other social phenomena.

In several important respects, Rigauer's theory seems to fit reality. His assessment of the conduct and nature of modern sport at the highest levels is not unreasonable. Sport at the top *is* intensely competitive; training has been analysed and scientifically organized; records and results are over-emphasized. Sport has for many become work. The events at Newcastle, New South Wales, on the recent England cricket tour to Australia could hardly be bettered as an illustration of the way in which the professional sports player sees his play as work. The managements of England and New South Wales had agreed that, should the match end early on the third day, an extra 25-over-a-side game would be put on for the benefit of the paying customers. 'Early' was defined as before 2.30 p.m. Both sides clearly collaborated to ensure a finish shortly after the prescribed time.

It is the rigidity of Rigauer's theory, however, which eventually undermines it. In the end there seem too many empirical objections. For example, Rigauer is almost addicted to quoting the famous American exponent of scientific management, F. W. Taylor, and making the parallel with sport. 'Up to now, personality came first; from now on, organization and system take over.'[1] But the sporting reality is surely a continuing tension and struggle between the two in which the balance shifts first one way, then the other. One could in fact argue that one of sport's attractions is the way in which organization and system are continually confronted by the more spontaneous forces which personality represents. Again, it does not seem sensible to say, as Rigauer does, that teamwork produces a set place for every player who has specialized and prescribed tasks, where arbitrary decisions, i.e. the scope for individual initiative, are no longer possible. This is certainly not true of the most popular team sports in either West or East.

Rigauer is prepared to admit that there exists for the individual athlete, in contrast to the industrial worker, the possibility of some degree of independence. But he insists that top-level sports permit self-development only within certain boundaries: 'the narrower the limits of any given system of athletic behaviour, the less the chance for self-realization. There is little tolerance for the individual shaping of a 100 metre dash.' But the 100 metres can surely provide plenty of opportunity for self-realization.

Another interesting issue raised by Rigauer is the function of sport in relation to labour power. Although recreational sport may not be quite so well stocked with alienating characteristics as top-level sport, it none the less buttresses the existing social order by its emulation and worship of the sporting élite. Moreover, participation in recreational sport improves the health of workers and so benefits industrial production. In other words – in fact in Rigauer's – it raises the level of labour power. But sport has sometimes proved an irritant to the forces of production, if not a major challenge. When workers took time off to watch midweek cup-ties management did not like it and some were sacked. But increasingly in the twentieth century a compromise was negotiated whereby men were allowed time off provided they made it up later. On such occasions sport seemed to be shaping work rather than the other way round. Floodlights, of course, largely removed the need for such arrangements.

Rigauer's emphasis on recreational sport as an aid to labour power shows that he believes it is largely workers who take part in sport. But empirical evidence from Europe, the United States and the British Isles suggests that it is the affluent who are more likely to participate in sport and whose health, therefore, presumably benefits. As Guttmann noted for

America, so we must accept for Britain: 'the disproportionate participation of the socially advantaged grows more pronounced as one moves up the scale of achievement from casual, recreational sports to top-level sports'. Perhaps the idea of sport as another form of capitalist repression has to be modified: sport aids the health of the entrepreneur, not only refreshing the body but also encouraging competitiveness and aggression!

Constructing theories of sport is obviously a worthwhile exercise if for no other reason than that it compels at least some of those heavily involved in sport to look closely at the assumptions which they make about it, especially in a country such as Britain where the notion that sport has nothing to do with anything else has a long and revered history as well as an extremely energetic present. Rigauer sees society as domination by one set of values which are largely unquestioned. But such a view does not seem to fit the complexities of the actual world. Another neo-Marxist, Horkheimer, offers a more hopeful view of the future of sport: 'sport is like art, literature and philosophy, and all the springs of the productive imagination. To preserve its freedom, to allow it to make its own decisions and dictate its own regulations, in spite of all the powerful influences from outside, seems to be the historic task of all those who are seriously concerned with sport'. As John Hoberman has so elegantly pointed out, sport does not necessarily belong to the world of unfreedom. It remains an area of ambiguity, a world to win.

Two sociological theories of sport and its place in society have been discussed briefly. These theories are almost certainly unfamiliar to most of the population; none the less portions of them may well have entered the wider culture in the same way that Shakespearian quotations have done. Such ideas often punctuate regular discourse on the subject without the user knowing their origin. Let us now turn to the significance of sport on a much more concrete level. We want to discover who plays what, how that has changed over time, what facilities are available, and what value people place on playing a particular sport or sports.

[77]

In the 1930s, 750,000 young and not-so-young men were playing football and there were even 75,000 playing members of tennis clubs. Some of the reality of the numbers playing or wishing to play sport was recognized by bodies such as the National Playing Fields Association and the London County Council, both of whom collected evidence which suggested that the availability of more facilities would boost the number of regular players even further.

On the other hand, in these days when local authorities spent £781 million on sport and leisure facilities in 1981–2, when there is a Sports Council and a Minister of Sport as well as powerful sports departments at the BBC and ITV and sports pages in every newspaper, it is worth noting that while there were 6.3 million members of sporting bodies in 1983, 48.5 million remained outside them. Perhaps that majority agree with the late Billy Butlin, the pioneer of holiday camps, who once said that when he felt like taking exercise he went for a lie-down until the feeling wore off.

Sport then, remains a minority activity, albeit a large minority. But what is played by whom and what changes have taken place over the last fifty years? It is obvious that social environment is very important in determining participation patterns. Age, sex, occupation, education, income, ethnic origin, upbringing and attitude all play a part in deciding what, if anything, will be played. In the 1930s it would not have been too difficult for a reasonably well-informed observer to characterize Britain's participatory sports in terms of class by virtue of the social composition of most of the participants. Football was working class, a game centred on the North, the Midlands and London. Rugby Union was middle class with working-class islands, most notably in South Wales but also in places like Leicester and Coventry. Rugby League was working class and so was boxing. Coarse fishing was largely working class too, like snooker and darts. Golf and tennis, on the other hand, were largely middle class, certainly in England. In Scotland, golf had a more popular clientele. Squash courts were unheard of outside public schools, universities and middle-class clubs. Cricket, track and field athletics and swimming were largely middle class, but again with significant working-class exceptions, such as the cricket leagues of the Midlands and the North.

Participation in sport, therefore, went with class lifestyle, and region or locality. A fascinating recent study has tended to confirm these basic associations between sport and class for more recent times. John Bale in *Sport and Place : A Geography of Sport in England, Scotland and Wales* (1982) showed that tennis, for example, had doubled its number of serious participants from 75,000 in the late 1930s to 150,000 by about 1980 but that it remained a suburban, middle-class, and largely southern game. A per capita index of tennis clubs showed that Surrey, Kent, Buckinghamshire and Oxfordshire all had more tennis clubs per head of population than Britain as a whole. Other largely southern and suburban sports are badminton, which grew by 60 per cent in less than a decade during the 1970s, table tennis and squash.[2] Squash may have had as many as 1.75 million players by the beginning of the 1980s. It will be interesting to see whether the popularity of racquet sports eventually spreads to the less well off and facilities begin to be placed away from the prosperous South and Midlands and away from largely suburban locations.

Bale also confirmed Scotland as the continued stronghold of golf. The Lothians and the Borders have five times the national average per capita number of golf clubs, with Dumfries, Galloway and Tayside having over four times the national average.[3] In cricket two old patterns of participation persisted: Kent, Surrey, Oxfordshire, Cambridgeshire, Sussex and Essex, all south-eastern counties, each having almost twice the national average number of clubs. Yorkshire maintained its traditional leadership in terms of participation, with over four and a half times the national average number of clubs; a leadership not reflected in the performance of the county side in the national championship.

It is not altogether clear how strong the link is between facilities for sport and excellence in sporting performance. But it *is* clear that without facilities, participation, at whatever level of achievement, is difficult, especially in an organized way. Local authorities had been able to spend the rate-payers' money on public parks and pleasure grounds from the middle of the nineteenth century. But parks tended to be decorous places of laid out gardens and formal walks unsuitable for boisterous sports. In Manchester, for example, in the 1870s, only bowls and tennis of a lukewarm nature were allowed and then only in some parks. Some school-boards, notably in Birmingham and London, were active in the provision of grounds for cricket and football, usually on the initiative of teachers. Local Education Authorities took on this mantle along with all the other school-board responsibilities in 1903. The 1907 Public Health Acts Amendment Act illustrated the progress made by mentioning cricket and football specifically for the first time and 'any other games or recreation' as being suitable activities on which the monies of local authorities might be spent, and in the years which were to elapse before the Second-World-War public funding of this kind was to reach record levels. The Miners Welfare Fund, a product of the Mining Industry Act of 1920, also led to an increase of sports facilities in the coalfields. But many contemporaries did not feel that it was enough. The National Playing Fields Association was a voluntary organization, set up in 1925 'to secure adequate playing fields for the present and future needs of all sections of the community'. (The Ancient Order of Frothblowers donated £1,050.) Its aim was to create 6 acres of playing space per thousand of the population, on which could be housed one football pitch, one junior football pitch or one hockey pitch, one cricket pitch, one three-rink bowling green, two tennis courts together with a small children's playground and a pavilion. Although it provided many new playing fields, it too could never match facilities with demand, and the lack of facilities, both indoor as well as outside, has struck all postwar investigators of British sport. The Birmingham University Physical Education Department, for example, was especially affronted to discover, in 1954, that only 47 public and 83 private cinder athletic tracks existed in England and Wales, whereas Sweden had 800 and Finland 500, both catering for much smaller populations.[4]

It was in the context of these discoveries, together with a series of humiliating blows to Britain's sporting self-respect at the highest international levels by a succession of defeats by the representatives of smaller and/or weaker countries, which prompted the Central Council of Physical Recreation (CCPR) to establish its committee of inquiry into sport under the Chairmanship of Sir John Wolfenden in 1957. The aim was to persuade central government to spend more on sport. The fact that the Albermarle Committee on the Youth Service also reported in 1960 and that National Service was about to end undoubtedly contributed to increased receptiveness in some high places. Wolfenden's Committee, given its anxiety about state control, did not recommend a Ministry of Sport. Only the British Communist Party were in favour of that in 1960. Wolfenden's idea of a Sports Development Council was taken up enthusiastically by Labour and included in their manifesto for the general election of 1964. When Labour won, the setting up of the Sports Council was an early fulfilment of this promise. In ex-Football League referee Denis Howell, Labour appeared to have the ideal man to monitor the needs of sport and he became Joint Parliamentary Under-Secretary in the Department of Education and Science with special responsibility for sport. Ten years later, in 1974, he was elevated to the position of Minister of State with Responsibility for the Environment, Water Resources and Sport – in effect a Minister for Sport. Hardly an echo was heard of Wolfenden's earlier anxieties.

The role of the Sports Council was to foster co-operation between the various voluntary bodies who ran individual sports and those more general institutions such as the CCPR and the British Olympic Association. It could only advise the Government on matters relating to the development of amateur sport and physical recreation. The Council did not really emerge as an independent entity with its own Royal Charter until 1971. Its aims were grand, if suitably vague. They were 'to develop and improve knowledge and practice of sport, play and recreation in the interest of social welfare and the enjoyment of leisure, among the public at large and to encourage high standards'. Perhaps there was a hint of tension there between a desire to provide everyone with the facilities and opportunity to play the sport of their choice, to whatever standard, and a policy to promote excellence and high standards of performance so that British sporting heads could be held high in the stadia of the increasingly international world of sport.

So far as participation was concerned the newly chartered Sports Council wasted no time. In 1972 it launched its campaign of Sport for All (the Council of Europe had instigated a similar venture ten years before). The aim was to increase participation and to persuade public and government that the provision of sport ought to be a social service, not quite on the crucial lines of housing, hospitals and schools, but unequivocally in the same area of responsibility.

From the vantage point of the late 1980s it is difficult to know how to evaluate so ambitious, and in an obvious sense so illusory, an aim. But a recent fascinating study, sponsored by the Sports Council, does have some pertinent things to say.[5] After a decade of Sport for All, facilities had improved, especially indoor ones like sports centres (27 in 1972, 770 in 1981) and swimming pools. Participation had increased too but mainly among the already active. Sport for All had failed to make much impact on those groups who were traditionally not sports players: school-leavers, ethnic minorities, low-income groups, the elderly and women. In this respect Britain is part of a Western European wide phenomenon where women participate less than men, older people less than younger, the semi-skilled and unskilled less than the professional, managerial and skilled. Even more disappointingly, participation rates among the unemployed have fallen. Those among the police, members of the armed services and students have risen and, significantly, car-owners were more active in sport than those without their own transport.

The relationship between social environment, lifestyle and patterns of participation in sport seems increasingly clear. Sport cannot escape the economic and social divisions of British society. Mark Shaw took an interesting look at participation in sport and leisure activities by combining the eleven neighbourhood types developed at the Centre for

Environmental Studies with the British Market Research Bureau's Target Index Data. In the pamphlet which he produced for the Sports Council in 1984 he tells us that golf-playing rises with neighbourhood status, save in Scotland, and that tennis remains a middle-class, suburban pursuit, and for the youthful rather than the young. Nor is it surprising to have confirmed that working-class leisure pursuits, including sport, remain predominantly male, whereas more middle-class sports are notably much more open to women. Football, snooker, darts, fishing, boxing and speedway, are quite firmly on the one side; tennis, badminton, sailing, camping, ten-pin bowling, table-tennis and show-jumping on the other.

The Sports Council itself obviously felt that the aims of Sport for All had not been achieved when it published *Sport in the Community: The Next Ten Years* (1982). The goal this time was to have one in three of the population involved in some kind of sporting activity by 1992. The main target groups were the 13–24-year-olds and the 45–59-year-olds. It seems unlikely now that lack of facilities in the right places is the major problem. As McIntosh and Charlton have pointed out, it is crèches at sports centres, improved public transport, perhaps better and more persistent advertising which might boost the numbers of players although it must be doubtful whether the numbers can be increased very significantly in an economy where 12–15 per cent unemployment appears to have become the norm.

Middle-class participation in sport has been particularly boosted since 1970 by the dissemination of medical findings showing the positive connection between exercise and health, and, especially, the association between high levels of physical activity and a low incidence of coronary heart disease. As Ralph S. Paffenbarger Jr. noted in the *New England Journal of Medicine* (May 1980), the public had begun to educate itself about the value of exercise both with and without the guidance of the medical profession. In Britain the Government have been drawing attention to the medical benefits of sport at least since 1975 and in 1977 the Sports Council, in association with the Health Education Council

[83]

and the BBC, began a campaign on the benefits of regular exercise with the cheery title of 'Feeling Great'. 'Come Alive' followed in 1978–9, encouraging individuals to take regular exercise. In general, though, sport seems to have been only one factor contributing to an enhanced 'health awareness' of the population. As McIntosh and Charlton point out, 'the growth of health clubs, aerobic classes and fitness clinics . . . the sale of books on diet and alternative medicine' were all pulling in the same direction. That a widespread desire to keep fit has had an impact on participation in sport is clear even if its exact nature is not.

Jogging, running, squash, badminton and swimming have experienced considerable growth although the growth is not easy to measure. It is also a growth which has hardly been steady over the population as a whole. Mark Shaw found that jogging and squash attracted the same, largely middle-class, people. Squash, for example, was heavily concentrated in high-status, non-farming residential areas 'where affluent and hectic urban lifestyles and concerns for health and status reach a peak'. Jogging, too, was very popular in urban middle-class neighbourhoods as a relatively relaxed and enjoyable way to stay fit and healthy. Its advantages were obvious. It required no special facilities, could be done any time, and did not demand a partner or a team. The growth in the entries for the London Marathon gives some statistical measure of the development of running. There were 7,747 accepted entries in 1981 and 19,735, out of over 50,000 applications, in 1983. Two years later there were over 70,000 applications for the 22,000 places.

Perhaps more surprisingly, more people are playing football in the mid-1980s than ever before and this at a time when the decline in support for the professional game among spectators accelerated. There are now about 1.6 million regular players in Great Britain. There were 25,000 clubs affiliated to the FA in 1966; almost 40,000 in 1979.[6] Sheffield alone in 1980 had 20,000 men and youths playing regularly and 200 registered clubs within a 20 mile radius of the city.[7] These players are heavily concentrated in the more severely deprived high-rise districts of the major cities and in the main areas of council housing. This is not surprising. But there are also significant concentrations in high-status neighbourhoods with relatively young age structures, such as those parts of inner cites where many young, single and affluent males live and those areas of modern family housing for white-collar workers. Perhaps this is explained by Mark Shaw's suggestion that 'playing football combines some of the characteristics of the "healthy" and perhaps rather middle-class participatory sports, with the characteristics of a working-class game'. This appears to be supported by additional evidence which suggests that a higher proportion of males in the 11–40 age group play football in the South of England than in the North although this probably has as much to do with affluence as class.[8] If the professional game remains a northern product in terms of the location of most of the clubs and spectators and the production of most of the players, the locus of recreational football is further south. Bale found that the only county in England with twice the national average of clubs per capita was Lincolnshire, followed by Northants, Essex, Cornwall and Surrey.[9]

One sport whose increase in popularity has surely owed little to the concern for health is snooker. Figures drawn from the General Household Survey suggest that participation, across the population as a whole, increased by 7 per cent between 1970 and 1980. As it was a male-dominated activity, participation might have been as high as 13 per cent of the male population. Although it remains a game dominated by the working-class male, there is just a hint that the attentions of television, crucial in the game's recent growth, is pushing it gently towards a more middle-class market.

In general, then, it would appear that sport has benefited from the widely publicized connection between exercise and health. But there is another side to this participatory explosion which may have even more dramatic effects on sport in the long run. Most sport is competitive. One does not have to accept totally the views of Veblen or Rigauer to agree with Anthony Powell that games are an outlet for power and aggression – 'You played a game to demonstrate that you did it better than someone else.'[10] It was an American football coach of the 1960s, Vince Lombardi of the Green Bay Packers, who coined the aphorism that winning is not the most important thing: it is the only thing. Round about the same time a British version was being circulated. Characteristically a little less serious, credit for its invention is given to the late Bill Shankly, the manager of Liverpool Football Club. 'Football isn't life and death,' he is alleged to have said, 'it is much more important than that.' It is astonishing how easily originality can be transformed into cliché. Donald Trelford ended his book on snooker, published in 1986, by quoting from a conversation with a leading player: 'I thought I was writing a book about snooker. Now I find I'm writing about life and death.' 'Oh no,' one of them laughed, 'it's much more important than that.' Top sporting men and women in Britain have increasingly subscribed to the view that winning is, if I may be permitted another sporting cliché, what it's all about. It was not always so.

When organized sport developed in the second half of the nineteenth century it did so on the basis of an ethic of sportsmanship which came out of the aristocratic public schools and attempted to envelop all who played and even those who looked on. Winning was not the important thing, but taking part. Team games in particular were to mould the characters of those individuals exposed to them by inculcating habits of co-operation and sacrifice. Individuality was allowed expression but in a context of group concerns. In one of the most oft-repeated phrases of the twentieth century, it did not matter whether you won or lost but how you played the game. Interestingly enough Grantland Rice, who was responsible for the phrase, was an American. 'For when the One Great Scorer comes, To write against your name, He marks – not that you won or lost – but how you played the game.'[11] One of the more respectable reasons for opposing professionalism was that sport should not be like work. Work was about winning, seriousness and profits; it was about getting on and ruthless competition. It was, without doubt, the business of life, as philosophers like Karl Marx and William Morris, for example, frequently reminded their readers. Sport was claimed as a relief from all that, a recreation for body and mind, a pause for enjoyment. More practically it also made the individual fitter for the more important tasks.

Certain caveats are, of course, required. Sport developed during the fag end of the golden age of rational recreation. In other words it was essential to provide it with a purpose, or a social function. To play sport had to be improving of both individual and society, even though one might like to play for the sake of it or for fun, and that was how you were supposed to play. The earlier idea that games (and therefore what we have come to call sport) were for children and not adults was expiring and their justification had to be firmly grounded in the nineteenth-century world of material benefit. Sport should not be a man's vocation or business, but it should help to keep him fit for what was his business.

A second caveat is that although the aristocratic ideal permeated all other classes, especially the middle ones, there was often a gap between ideal and reality, a gap which its supporters found difficult to acknowledge or were prepared to overlook. Nowhere is this more clear than among the establishment enthusiasts of cricket. In the public schools it was cricket above all which fostered manliness and leadership. It was more than a game; it was an institution shot through with desirable moral qualities. It was a welder together of colonies like Australia and, for some enthusiasts, the cement of Empire itself. Indeed, cricket has often been called an art by its devotees. It was Britain's unique and wonderful gift to world culture, to be linked with parliamentary democracy and the sandwich. It was only a pity that more of the world did not adopt it. Nor did this respect for cricket disappear in 1914 with the society that spawned it. Forty years later, R. A. Butler, then Chancellor of the Exchequer, exempted cricket from entertainment tax (hardly surprising some cynics might say) because it occupied 'a special place among sports, not only as forming a part of the English tradition, but as a common interest helping to bind together the various countries of the Commonwealth'. As Derek Birley rather acidly pointed out in *The Willow Wand* (1979), cricket took on board the social values of Britain's ruling establishment, increasingly becoming the focus of upper-class nostalgia for a past golden age in which not only did Britain consist of a society in which everyone had a place, but one where everyone knew they had a place and kept to it.

It has been mentioned before, however, that both cricket and cricketers often failed to live up to the ideal. W. G. Grace, for example, was in many respects the epitome of the English sporting hero but he could be as irritatingly fallible as, say, Ian Botham, though unlike Botham he usually escaped censure and always escaped punishment. Grace often ignored the so-called spirit of the game if it suited his interests, taking lavish expenses while remaining an amateur and enjoying an amateur's privileges. He intimidated umpires and, above all, hated losing, doing all that he could, often going well beyond the boundaries of sharp practice, to avoid defeat. P. A. Perrin reported that during a Gentlemen v. Players match Grace said to him, 'You're going in with me first next time, young 'un. Now be sure to have very long nails put into your boots, and take care to run up and down the pitch to ruin it. That is our only chance of winning the match. They would be suspicious of me, but would never dream of you as new in cricket being up to such tricks.'

None the less the sportsmanship ideal remained a powerful one. Top-level football was professional after the mid-1880s and increasingly dominated on the playing side by working-class players who brought a more pragmatic and down-to-earth attitude to games and who were certainly determined to win − it was, as they often reminded people, their livelihood. But even there, playing to win was never allowed to become the dominant ideology. This was partly due to the fact that, like most sports up until the Second World War and indeed beyond, football was run by gentlemen who were steeped in the sportsmanship ethic and who were determined to keep the business side in check. No payment of directors, no unrestricted dividends, no free market for labour and no sponsorship were allowed. Football at the top may have been partly a business, and its critics were often unwilling to bestow upon it the honour of sport at all, but it was not run like one. Power, status, the obsessions of the fan, all contributed to the motives of the football-club directors, but they were not profit maximizers and they remained, like the magistrates, among the great unpaid, public benefactors – though perhaps more often without honour in their own communities. They did not run their clubs like they ran their businesses, often allowing good money to follow bad and not infrequently bearing considerable losses. It was not that football and business, or indeed sport and business, were expected to inhabit separate spheres. But each was expected to know its place and in sport business was the lesser partner.

In the last two decades or so, that balance has shifted. Business and its values have been winning the battle with sport and its values. The reasons for this shift are not difficult to explain, or at least to place in the context of social and economic change. Top-level sport has had its paying support seriously eroded since the ephemeral booms of the immediate postwar world. This is true of all the major spectator sports: athletics, cricket, football, rugby league and horse-racing. This would have presented less of a problem if it had not been accompanied by two other dramatic changes: the decline of the monied amateurs, which first changed the face of top-level cricket and is now radically altering athletics, and the removal of restrictions on the earning power of players, first and very dramatically in football. The result has been the classic bind of falling revenue and rising costs. The bureaucracies of the sporting world have a vested interest in survival and they have turned to the one source of financial support which appears to offer not just salvation but affluence – business. This would probably have been less available without the spread of television. Access to every home has prompted all forms of business to use top-level sport as a means of promoting their products. And they are increasingly prepared to pay handsomely for the privilege.

So, as attendances fall, the money available to the best practitioners has dramatically increased. Earnings of even the rather less than best can be very considerable, as the 1985 salary of the Sunderland manager most graphically demonstrated. He reportedly earned as much as £164,000 in that year even though his club only escaped relegation to the third division in the last match of the season. But the winners do best, and the rewards for winning even single events can be very large. In 1984 the British Open Golf champion won a title first competed for in 1860: but he also won £70,000. The men's singles champion at Wimbledon took home £100,000, the winning Derby jockey £20,000 and the Liverpool football team £7,000 a man for missing one penalty less than Roma in the European Cup Final. John Lowe received £115,000 for a nine-dart finish and the Welsh winner of the Chicago Marathon was rewarded with 95,000 dollars, 50,000 of which were for breaking the world record for the distance. Also in 1984 the snooker player Steve Davis was said to have earned, or received, £1 million, of which only 20 per cent came directly from the game.

With such sums at stake it is not surprising that among leading sportsmen and women attitudes to winning appear to have hardened and the rhetoric and ideology which emphasizes the value of winning regularly dominates the sporting pages of the press and the programmes on radio and television. Only losing receives more sensational coverage than winning. And yet, apparently at the moment of its greatest triumph, the notion that winning is the most important thing has begun to take some knocks. Jogging and running have emphasized taking part, getting into condition, running against yourself and the clock. The competitive element has been played down and often deliberately attacked. Sport is for fitness and enjoyment and competition is not essential to either. Perhaps most crucial for the traditional team games these ideas have appeared in the schools, where sport has been increasingly criticized as obsessed with winning and the production of champions. Rather than play a team game, children should study the components of body management so that they can work out an appropriate exercise routine to keep them fit for the life they lead. There is also evidence that many boys and girls do not like competitive sport. Research sponsored by the Physical Education Association of Great Britain and the Sports Council established a positive correlation between mental ability and success in competitive school sports. The less able were less successful and apparently found sport increasingly unattractive. In addition, a survey carried out in the late 1960s asked people to place, in order of importance, five attractions of taking part in sport: 'pleasure of competition, keeping fit, the chance to mix with other people, getting out in the open air and taking your mind off other things'. Pleasure of competition was placed fourth by males and last by females. Males in full-time education placed it first, while females so employed placed it last. Such research is difficult to interpret but the conclusions of McIntosh and Charlton on this matter seems to suggest that competitive sport in schools is going to have to fight harder for its place in the future and may attract fewer followers. Clearly competitive sport has a strong, if limited following; but perhaps not strong enough to justify its domination of the school curriculum especially in the form of team games.

   Dislike of competitive sport and the growth of alternatives to it may be combining to undermine team games in the schools. Comprehensive reorganization has been underpinned by the principle that all children should be encouraged to identify their interests and fulfil their potential. This has meant that opportunities should be provided for participation in as wide a range of physical and sporting activities as resources will allow. As in the wider world outside, there are now many other competitors for student time, energy and commitment than the traditional track and field, cricket, football and rugby. The idea that a wider choice of sports should be available has also been buttressed by research discussed earlier linking regular exercise with improved health. But there is another threat to competitive school sport. Physical educationists have also been pointing out that their subject no more escapes cuts in government spending than any other. Normally the physical education curriculum would be made up of two strands. The first would be a physical education (PE) and games spot on the timetable of all pupils. The second would be voluntary, extra-curricular activities participated in by the most able and based on school teams. Diminishing resources have had the effect of reducing teachers' time and school capitation money spent on these so-called extra-curricular activities. The available money has to be used first to meet the cost of the activities of all pupils. Teachers themselves, their salaries low, their resources cut, their efforts and difficulties apparently unappreciated by government, are increasingly reluctant to give up time and energy for unpaid coaching and supervision. And early in 1986 DES Regulation 909 appeared to exacerbate the seriousness of an already critical situation by allowing local education authorities to sell off school playing fields. One estimate, admittedly from the sports lobby, put 450, under threat in the spring of 1986.

Cricket has been particularly severely hit by these changes. It requires time to play outside school hours and decent pitches to play on. Both have been disappearing in the state schools. Grammar schools usually had a sporting tradition based on their imitation of the public schools where games were compulsory. This meant not only possession of their own playing fields but the employment of full-time groundsmen to tend them – crucial in the preparation of the cricket pitch. Many comprehensives do not possess their own playing fields and even where they do they are looked after, if that is the phrase, by a few rigidly time-controlled workmen employed by the Council centrally to go the rounds of all parks and education department responsibilities. The result has been that top-level cricket in the Britain of the 1980s has moved back towards the social profile of earlier times. By the early 1960s professionals had long dominated the game, and they came mostly from working- or lower-middle-class backgrounds and grammar school educations. Ex-public schoolboys in the test team were becoming a rarity, usually only the captain. But in 1985 David Gower was captaining an England cricket XI in which seven out of eleven were public school educated. England cricket could become entirely dependent on the products of the public schools and the private day schools, both of which continue to value participation in traditional team games and have the money to maintain it.

All this demands that competitive sport looks closely at itself and examines those values which have increasingly underpinned it and been a dominant theme since the end of the Second World War. As newspapers and television continue to worship winners in a society in which most of the rewards go to the strong – notions further popularized and legitimated by Thatcherism – the non-competitive empire is striking back. Competitive sport in general and team games in particular are being rejected by large numbers of people. Tales of high salaries and drug-taking may also be turning people away. It's nice to be a winner, but it is not the only or the most important consideration. Most people, after all, are losers and without all those losers there would be no winners. Thomas Fuller wrote in 1732 that it was a silly game where nobody wins. The Americans in particular would agree because they do not allow draws in any of their major sports and go into 'overtime' to prevent them. Winning does have a lot to commend it. But it needs to be kept in perspective. Victorian and Edwardian sporting values were generously laced with hypocrisy from which the later twentieth century has determined to distance itself. But the ideal of sportsmanship is worth something. The fact that we have shed the hypocrisy does not mean that we have got the balance right.

# 4
# Comparisons

This chapter will compare the involvement of the state in sport in different countries since 1914. It will focus mainly on how and why the British state became involved in British sport in the twentieth century and make comparisons with the role of the state in sport elsewhere. Germany, Italy and the Soviet Union will be specifically referred to for the period 1918–39 and some attempt will be made to explain the sporting prowess, already briefly noticed, of East Germany in the years after the Second World War.

The state's involvement with what in Britain has long been the epitome of voluntary activity undoubtedly flowed from sport's growing international connections. Britain played a leading creative role in establishing sport in the international arena. By the end of the nineteenth century test cricket matches between England and Australia had become eagerly anticipated events in the relatively new sporting calendar. Cricket teams also visited America and football tours to Europe were about to begin in earnest. By 1914 both codes of rugby were played at international level and the first international football matches between teams from outside the British Isles were taking place. The modern Olympic movement had begun and sports like boxing, which had long had a transnational character, were beginning to list world champions at a variety of weights. In all sports the number of competing countries doubled between the 1900s and 1920s and doubled again between the 1920s and 1950s.

In such circumstances the first sporting nation found itself, in sport, subject to intense competition, similar to that beginning to be felt in trade and industry. The signs were there quite early. Test matches were lost to the Australians. In 1895 a London Athletic Club team, containing much of the cream of British amateur talent, failed to win a single event in a match against the New York Athletic Club. British performances in the Olympic Games of 1908 and 1912 disappointed many commentators, with, in 1908, the Americans doing much the best on the track and in the field at the newly built White City Stadium in Shepherds Bush. Moreover, the British reputation for fair play appeared suspect when British officials, on flimsy pretexts, disqualified an apparently victorious American in the 400 metres and attempted to help an exhausted Italian to gain the tape ahead of another American in the marathon. In Stockholm in 1912 Britain won only nine out of ninety-eight events, provoking sportsmen like F. A. M. Webster to note, sadly, that we were even being defeated by 'lesser European nations' who for generations past had been our pupils in all sports. The Duke of Somerset, Chairman of the British Olympic Council, complained after Stockholm that the fact had to be faced: British athletics was in a bad way. Our own national championships were regularly won by foreigners and colonials and we were far from always victorious at cricket and rugby. It was a time for cultural pessimism. The report of the Inter-Departmental Committee on Physical Deterioration (1904) was bandied about misleadingly, and was offered as evidence for a decline in the physical capabilities of the British race which our losses in sport seemed to confirm.

After the war, one of the parrot cries of press and commentator was 'back to normal'. Sport, and international sport at that, had an increasingly important role to play in that normality. The hardening of international relations produced by the war and its aftermath, together with the expansion in

[95]

the numbers of British sportsmen travelling abroad, was bound to stimulate Foreign Office interest. At any rate, from 1921 'Sport' begins to appear as a separate entry in the subject index of their files.

In the first place, the Foreign Office was involved in the increasing number of practical problems which surrounded the visits of British athletes abroad. Arrangements had to be made, permission had often to be obtained, information had to be exchanged by recognized and responsible representatives in the new and more complex post-Versailles world.

It was also increasingly clear that the role of sport had to be monitored and data collected if relationships with countries based on real knowledge and awareness were to be built. And because Britain was the first sporting nation, its sporting organization and achievements were of great interest elsewhere in the world. The Foreign Office was often asked in the 1920s to provide details of how British sport was run, by, for example, Romania, the Dutch and a number of countries in the Middle East and Latin America. In such circumstances even the Foreign Office could hardly fail to recognize that sport was a part of British culture that interested other nations. It might, therefore, play a role in establishing or maintaining British influence in those countries. There was even some suggestion in Germany that British stamina and good nerves during the First World War had been due to British sport, notably in a famous book by Rudolf Kircher, *Fair Play: The Games of Merrie England* (1928).

Finally, in a world which saw international sport expanding its empire and a sporting world that witnessed rapid improvements in the standard of performance by previously unheralded countries – all emblazoned across newspapers which gave more and more space to the reporting of sport – the association of sporting standards with national prestige seemed undeniable. As early as 1921 British residents in Barcelona complained about the inferior displays of visiting British football teams. Criticisms of British footballers came from Denmark in the north and Portugal in the south. By 1928 the British Consul in Turin was warning his Whitehall superiors that there was no point in going to play football there without the strongest possible team allied to the firmest possible resolve. Especially when abroad the British sportsman had to behave well, as well as play well, and it was the duty of the Foreign Office to remind people who needed reminding about the nature of their responsibilities.

Of course, part of the reason for this new concern was the way in which sport was not only being fervently embraced by foreigners but was being used by the new totalitarian states for propagandist purposes. In Britain, as we have seen, sport remained a voluntary activity. It is true that Pelham Warner, of all people, cricket journalist and greasy eminence at the MCC, had advocated the setting up of a Ministry of Sport in 1919 but there was no intention that the state should undertake the management of sport; rather that it should simply provide resources and general assistance. Warner's remarks have to be set in the context of the Bolshevist threat to Britain which some Conservatives professed to have identified in 1919. As Sir Robert Hadfield, the Sheffield steel magnate, said when opening the company's new playing fields in 1923, 'no one had ever heard of a good sportsman rising among the Socialists or the Bolshevists. Sport in itself was the best antidote to revolution and revolutionary ideas'. Moreover, foreign athletes were increasingly receiving state support while still competing as amateurs against British ladies and gentlemen who, in theory, only received expenses. The Argentine winner of the 1932 Olympic marathon had spent six months abroad preparing for the race. But it was the Fascists and Bolsheviks, especially Fascist Italy and Germany, who increasingly used sport for political ends. How could the British Government fail to respond?

The use of sports and athletic festivals for nationalistic purposes has a longer history than is often supposed. It certainly goes back to the gymnastic movements in Germany in the first half of the nineteenth century. As Hoberman has reminded us, the fusion of rhythmic bodies into a symbolic whole has become a standard element in the totalitarian liturgy. It signifies to the world, both inside and outside the performing nation, political unity. In the 1920s and 1930s it must have seemed a new and disturbing phenomenon,

[97]

especially to the British who had never gone in for such athletic symbolism. The Fascists found sport attractive in part because they were, in general, enthusiastic about the human body which they associated with instinct, spontaneity, power and male leadership. When depicted in personal form the state was usually given a muscular physique rather than a more reflective, thinking persona.

Sports were lavishly subsidized in Mussolini's Italy and assiduously promoted from the mid-1920s. Sport seemed to offer so many advantages: at home it could act as mixer, leveller and distractor, as well as being a relatively inexpensive and speedy way of building up physical fitness and national cohesion for a government that insisted that the nation must be prepared for war. Abroad, sporting involvement and especially success at the highest level could be used to demonstrate both the heroic qualities and the vitality of all the people under their new and progressive state. In Italy the Olympic successes of 1932 and 1936 were hailed as proof of national supremacy, as was the World Cup victory of 1934. (Italy's victory was due, according to supporters of the regime, to 'the masculine energies of a bursting vitality within our Mussolini's Italy'.) England refused to take part in the World Cup having fallen out with the International Federation of Football Associations (FIFA) over the proper definition of 'amateur'.

Sport in Mussolini's Italy was promoted by the state on two levels. The most skilful players of the most popular sports received considerable state and commercial backing. The Olympic teams and the new national soccer league were clearly in this category. The Fascist Sports Charter of 1929 gave the Italian Olympic Committee the job of running Italian sport at the highest level. The second, and lower, level of sports' promotion concerned those sports which were thought of primarily as mass participation events, *bocce* (an Italian variant of bowls), chess, tug of war and gymnastics. These were to be the responsibility of the Fascist leisure department, OND (Opera Nazionale Dopolavoro), known as Dopolavoro.[1] It is clear now that this Fascist attempt at 'sport for all' was far from a total success. But what was clear enough at the time was the use to which top-level sport was being put by the Italian government. By the mid-1930s the new Nazi regime in Germany was making even more effective use of sport as a propaganda weapon.

Imperial Berlin had been scheduled to stage the Olympic Games in 1916. A leading German sports organizer, Carl Diem, had visited the USA and been impressed by the facilities and coaching he had found there. One of the later results of this was the expansion of sport in the secondary schools of the Weimar Republic with a corresponding growth in facilities and especially new stadiums. It was this start that the Nazis were able to expand. The Athletic Nation State was a proclaimed Nazi ideal. A Reich Sportsführer was appointed within the Ministry of the Interior and he took over the presidency of the German Olympic Committee.

In some respects the 1936 Berlin Olympics was both a justification of Germany's recent sporting history and a propaganda success for the Nazi regime. The story of the Olympics is well known and cannot be repeated here. It is told in the greatest detail by Richard Mandell in *The Nazi Olympics* (1972). Suffice it to say that signs of anti-Jewish prejudice inside Germany were temporarily removed and the movement, especially strong in the United States, to boycott the Games was thwarted. At least one leading British competitor at the Games wondered whether it was all worth it in such a context, but Philip Noel Baker, former Olympic athlete better known as a Labour MP, assured him that it was!

Even before the Olympics, Britain's sporting relations with Germany had been questioned when an international football match was arranged between England and Germany at Tottenham in December 1935. The fixture provoked opposition from Jewish organizations, the TUC and the Communist Party and, in part, focused on the presence of visiting German supporters. One of its products was a pamphlet, written by the TUC General Secretary, Walter Citrine, on the way sport was used by the Nazis, emphasizing that sport was not socially or politically neutral. There was never any real chance that the game would be postponed. It is clear that the Foreign Office wished to avoid antagonizing Germany, whose supporters apparently behaved well before, during and after a comprehensive three-goal defeat.

It is interesting to compare the Foreign Office response to that game with their approach to the return match in Berlin in May 1938. Earlier that year Foreign Office policy had been articulated as one of discouraging football matches against foreigners. The FO certainly wished to discourage poor performances by inadequate teams that produced only embarrassment rather than prestige. It was clear that the Germans attached a great deal of importance to the coming match, with their team coming together for training and practice for several weeks. Such careful preparation was not a feature of English international football and the opinion was expressed that the FO should remind the FA of its responsibilities. Robert Vansittart wrote to the Secretary of the FA on 6 May and was assured by Stanley Rous that 'every member of the team will do his utmost to uphold the prestige of this country'. In the event the English team gave the Fascist salute before the match and also conceded three goals. But before 100,000 spectators – 400,000 had applied for tickets – they themselves scored six and won a famous victory which, the chaps in the FO thought, revived British sporting prestige in Germany.

After the Revolution of 1917 the Soviet Union, as we have already noted, made use of sport to improve the health and physical welfare of the population. There was some hostility to the competitive sports of capitalism, as there had been, for example, in the workers' sports movement of the German Social Democrats and as there was to be in the workers' sports movements of western and central Europe which flourished, briefly, in the years between the world wars. But by the 1930s the Soviet attitude to sport had undergone a considerable change. Encouragement and support were provided for the high achiever in athletics and other sports. Competition and the spectacular sporting performance were back in favour. By 1952 there was no doubt of the importance Stalin's Russia attached to sporting success – and failure. When the USSR lost to Yugoslavia in the qualifying round of the Olympic football tournament in that year, the

Generalissimo disbanded the team and ordered the players to be interrogated as suspected Tito agents.[2] Sport in the Soviet Union had come to have a similar function to that which it had in the capitalist west: to improve physical fitness, provide mass entertainment, gain support for the regime and build international prestige.

Sport remained the individual's business in Britain, but the examples from over the channel were dragging the British state into it, however hesitantly and reluctantly. Physical education in Germany, for example, was admired by influential administrators in this country. The Board of Education sponsored a visit by a British delegation in November 1936 and published its report as a pamphlet. Facilities in Germany were apparently both more varied and more numerous and the visitors detected a spirit abroad that got things done. But they were also able to identify the essential difference between the two countries. In Germany, the whole population was under a legal and moral obligation to prepare for physical fitness.[3] Could such compulsion work in Britain? Perhaps Germany was going too far in its emphasis on the physical condition of the body to the neglect of a more balanced approach in which intellectual considerations would have a clear place.

These examples from Europe made an important contribution to the renewed public debate about the physical condition of the population. What was happening in Germany and Italy was placed alongside the impact of the Depression and, in particular, the studies of men like John Boyd Orr on British standards of nutrition, most particularly in his controversial *Food, Health and Income : A Survey of Adequacy of Diet in Relation to Income* (1936). Out of these concerns came the Physical Training and Recreation Act of 1937, which, among other things, set up a National Fitness Council. In the event, the war overtook this attempt by the state to improve the nation's physical well-being, although it did result in increased public spending on facilities for sport. But the importance of these initiatives lies in what they reveal about influential opinion on the role of sport in society. Suggestions in German newspapers that the scheme was part of a compulsory sports programme brought vigorous denials from the Chairman of the National Fitness Council, Lord Aberdare. The NFC, he said, stood four square for a policy of which free choice and freedom from any kind of compulsion was the fundamental principle. The sole aim was to benefit the individual. There were no ulterior motives or hidden objectives, though of course it would be foolish to deny the hope that it would raise standards of corporate as well as personal conduct.

By 1939 the Foreign Office was much more alert to the place of sport in culture and propaganda than it had been in 1918 but neither the government nor the ruling élite of British sport wanted a state controlled system as seemed to be in place in the Fascist West and the Communist East. Some sporting authorities wanted government help, most notably athletics in Olympic years. The cost of preparation and transport was rising as the perception of the Olympics as a major international event grew. Moreover, the British Olympic movement, if not aristocratic to the core, was peopled by men who knew how to make the most of the influence they had. The British *Olympic Journal* for July 1931 reminded the nation's elected leaders that the country's efficiency could and would be judged by its performance in sport. This made it imperative that the best possible team be sent to the Los Angeles games the following year and the Government ought to offer support from the Exchequer. The Government accepted the arguments but shuffled its feet uneasily. The most it was prepared to do was sponsor the team which entered for the Schneider Trophy air races of 1927, 1929 and 1931. Such adventurousness could be justified on military grounds. In general, the Government, while recognizing its value to the national life, did little of a material kind to help sport. Meanwhile the Foreign Office, when deprived of Anglo–German football matches, could always perform a useful service by helping the Swedes to arrange broadcasting facilities for the English Cup Final and explaining to distinguished foreigners how difficult it was to obtain tickets for the match. They also smoothed ruffled Polish sensibilities after an English professional footballer spat at a referee after being ordered off for foul play before 50,000 Poles, including a marshal and a general. They were keen to establish cricket as the national sport in Afghanistan. The state professionalization of sport however, remained a road down which neither British government nor British sport wished to travel.

The problems associated with the relationship between sport and the state returned, however, with the Cold War. Once the Warsaw Pact countries re-entered international sport in the 1950s it was clear that sport, like many other aspects of life in the Eastern bloc, was financed and organized by the state. Moreover, it was indisputable that such state sponsorship of sport was successful on the one hand and useful in the prestige war on the other. Britain's sporting pride, meanwhile, took a whole series of knocks at just about everyone's hands and feet, including those of Communists. British sport seemed totally unfit to cope with a new world of either state sponsorship or the more or less unlimited financial support from business and education offered in countries like the United States. Britain dithered but, essentially, clung on to its gentlemanly notion of amateurism, its preference for voluntaryism, while making use of the occasional sporting hero who did emerge. In a sense the predicament of both British sport and its relationship to the British state in this period is neatly illustrated by the use which was made of one such sporting giant. The Foreign Office decided to send Roger Bannister – as everyone knows, the first man to run a mile in under four minutes – on a goodwill tour of the United States in 1954. It was accounted a smashing success: but some of Bannister's TV appearances had to be curtailed because they threatened to infringe his amateur status. There was, of course, no danger of the Foreign Office losing theirs.

Russia seemed to present the greatest sporting as well as the greatest political threat. From 1951 articles criticizing Russian attitudes to sport were commonplace. The titles are revealing: 'Putting the Spite into Sport', 'A Sports Parade for Communism' and 'Taking the Sport out of Sport'. The visit of the Moscow Dynamo Football team in 1945 had done little to improve sporting relations. But it was the rapidly growing sporting prowess of East Germany rather than the Soviet Union which astonished and irritated the West in general and Britain in particular. After all, Russia was a gigantic country and if it was determined to do well in the Olympics it had the resources to do it. But East Germany was small and not particularly rich: it had appeared to be the less-developed part of the divided country. How could such a country perform so well in athletics, in boxing, in gymnastics, in swimming? By the Montreal Olympics (1976) East Germany appeared to have become the most successful sporting nation, per capita, in the world. John Bale has attempted to place the 'world-class athletic productivity' of East Germany in comparative perspective. He counted the number of athletes who in 1976, achieved a performance in one of the standard Olympic events which ranked them in the top hundred in the world. He then related these absolute numbers to population to produce a per capita index. Finland topped the league with 31.4, followed by Trinidad with 22.25 and East Germany with 14.95. The United States scored 4.69, Britain 2.36 and the Soviet Union 2.56.[4]

Two important factors were probably responsible for providing the initial impetus for the development of sport in the German Democratic Republic. Perhaps the most vital was the concern of the Soviet Union to promote sport and physical education in its own zone of influence.[5] Sport would promote both fitness and enjoyment, thereby building a population capable of adapting to all kinds of military as well as civil work in a world divided between two apparently permanently opposed systems of political economy. Second, it cannot have been a hindrance to sport that Walter Ulbricht, the effective head of the Socialist Unity Party from 1946 to 1971, was a sports enthusiast. He had himself been a member of a workers' gymnastic club in the workers' sports movement of Weimar Germany. He saw that sport might form a model for 'performers' elsewhere in German society and, following the Soviet example, could provide one of the few ways by which the superiority of socialism might be demonstrated to the old west and the new south alike. 'Ubiquitous sport' also became a significant part of the government's strategy for coping with an unusually youthful population in the 1950s, a decade which saw many adults leave for the Federal Republic before the building of the Berlin Wall in 1961. That it was apparently so rapidly successful must be due in part to the fact that Germany had its own strong sporting tradition going back to the *Turnerverein* (gymnastic clubs) of the nineteenth century. Many types of modern sport, from gymnastics to tennis and athletics to football, were expanding in popularity during the Weimar Republic, and it was this development on which the Nazis had grafted their highly centralized sports organization.

These factors have all to be taken into account when attempting to cope with both the importance of sport in East German society and the success of their sportsmen and sportswomen, especially the sportswomen, in international competition. The question is how that success has been achieved and whether it offers a pattern which Britain could profitably follow.

Sport has had an important role at all levels of the educational system since the GDR was established. Both physical education and games have taken up a large proportion of secondary school time since the 1950s, as much as 10 per cent according to some estimates. Similarly all physically healthy university students were required to take part in sport for the first three years of their course. German trade unions also built up their own sports organizations. The role of sport in the army and the security police is well known and the Central Army Sports Club (Vorwarts), together with the Sports Club of the People's Police (Dynamo) have provided a steady stream of high-level sportsmen and women. A University of Physical Culture was established at Leipzig in 1950. Its main purpose was to train teachers of physical education, coaches and sports officials and to carry out research into all aspects of sport and physical education. It had over 2,000 students in 1975. Sports science was a reputable degree subject in the GDR long before it was in Britain. (Even now it is doubtful if it has achieved the status of more traditional courses of study in this country.)

Sports participation is actively encouraged among the

population as a whole and the state has provided good facilities. For a small sum anyone can join any sports club. One estimate (1979) claimed that such clubs had 2.6 million members or about 16 per cent of the population. These figures may be compared with the recent Sports Council estimates for Britain mentioned earlier which suggested a membership of about 11 per cent for sports organizations. It has been estimated that up to 40 per cent of the East German population make regular use of sports facilities.

Moreover, the widespread participation in sport is used in sophisticated ways to search for and develop the talent which will bring victory at the highest sporting level. Special sports schools have been in existence for over thirty years (there were twenty-two in 1959), where carefully selected pupils concentrate on improving their performance in a relatively narrow range of Olympic events. Since 1965 another medium for monitoring sporting talent has been the *Spartakiaden*, annual competitions on local, regional and eventually national levels. Most top athletes will have come over these hurdles and enjoy a relatively privileged existence distinguished by, for example, a higher standard of living, opportunities for foreign travel, enhanced status within the GDR and the possibility of further social mobility. They have ample time to train, excellent facilities and do not have any financial anxieties. Many are assigned to a small number of highly ranked clubs which concentrate on particular sports.

Finally, the GDR has invested a good deal of physical and intellectual resources in applying science to sport in order to improve performance. The importance of the University at Leipzig has already been mentioned in this connection. Sports medicine has been one area in which the GDR has been a particularly persistent and successful pioneer. Specialist doctors for sport were introduced in 1963 and one estimate puts their number at over 700 by 1980. Again this concern with finding out more about the human body, its strengths and limitations, and what it can do in certain circumstances is in a German tradition which goes back to the Weimar Republic at least. In the GDR it is an area of research still shrouded in some secrecy. But it has clearly played an important part in the rise of East Germany to sporting pre-eminence.

There is, of course, more to be said about this pre-eminence and how it has been achieved. It is, for example, partly the result of a concentration of effort in a restricted range of sports. Most of these were chosen with German traditions and the Olympics in mind. Track and field athletics, swimming, gymnastics, boxing, football and sports with military associations like shooting, riding and skiing are the ones in which East Germans have most notably excelled. Their presence in tennis, hockey, golf and rugby has been less spectacular.

Nor is it entirely clear that participation in sport in the GDR as a whole is at a significantly higher level than in Britain. The statistics relating to participation must be examined with caution. They are far from voluminous and what interpretation is placed on those which *are* available often seems to depend on subjective factors. But David Childs, a political scientist, does suggest that the GDR, far from having pushed popular participation in sport to levels well beyond those achieved in Britain, is beginning to face a not unfamiliar range of problems. For example, a 1968 survey of children aged 12–19 in Karl Marx Stadt shows that half did not pursue organized sport outside school hours. The most common explanation is that they had received bad marks in the compulsory sports lessons at school and had been correspondingly discouraged. Does this suggest that the rigorous search for champions at school had had adverse affects on the discarded majority? Again, a survey of adults in Karl Marx Stadt in 1965, shows that 37 per cent put sports or games first among *desired* leisure activities. But when a list was made of what the respondents actually did, sport was placed eighth behind such familiar activities as watching TV, reading, discussions and handicrafts. In the German Gymnastics and Sports Association in 1975, the most popular sports were football and fishing, which again makes it sound rather like Britain. Although the evidence suggests greater participation in sport in the GDR than in Britain, the gap is probably narrower than was once supposed. Perhaps David Childs is right when he concludes that 'a great many people in the GDR are not as enthusiastic about sport as the authorities would like them to be'. However, perhaps the state's insistence on the availability of time and facilities in the early years of life has been more successful in discovering and nurturing talent than the British state-aided voluntary system has been.

East German pre-eminence in a range of sports has often been crudely explained by the accusation that their athletes have used drugs. Female swimmers especially, notably after their successes in the Montreal Olympics, were alleged to be fed diets of steroids and male hormones in order to increase muscle bulk. The regimen in the sports schools was claimed to be tough and sinister, based on a mixture of drugs, vows of silence and children being the subject of experiments by high-performance theorists. The evidence for most of these allegations is thin and often comes from young athletes who have defected to the West. It does seem clear that a state-backed concern with the application of science in sports medicine could well have led to improved training methods and enhanced levels of performance. Some American theorists have suggested that Western athletes 'do not know how to train' and that individuals need to be screened at an early age so that body structure, metabolism and sport are matched in the optimum fashion. This may involve some restriction of individual choice.[6] As John Hoberman asked,[7] 'how far does one want and should one want to develop the combination of technology, medicine, training and athletes, in the area of sport, and where should the line be drawn?'

In Britain, the idea of athletes who are state-financed, state-trained and state-directed still remains anathema, which partly explains the resistance of the British Olympic Association to the Conservative government's attempt to persuade it to boycott the Moscow Olympics of 1980. Clearly the British state has become much more involved in the promotion and financing of sport in the last thirty years and probably few people would now object if the free market, with a little state aid, provided, for example, the facilities and therefore the opportunities of a specialist school as the first step on a ladder to sporting excellence. Certainly there has been little objection to the Lilleshall football experiment other than a disbelief in its efficacy.

# 5
# Conclusions

The Duke of Wellington never actually said that the Battle of Waterloo was won on the playing fields of Eton. But the myth is revealing of the perception of some Britons of their national character: that an essentially meaningless activity, the playing of games, so prepared the nation's élite, both physically and in terms of character, for sacrifice and leadership that it enabled the British to defeat the greatest military power in the world, build up a great empire in the nineteenth century and win two world wars. During the First World War British troops advanced towards the German trenches kicking footballs of both shapes, round and oval. The German Army had adopted football shortly before 1914 because it was supposed to help in the preparation of martial virtues. Perhaps they should have done it earlier. In the interwar years the British victory in the war was firmly associated with the country's addiction to sport and games, and as other countries sought our secret, the Foreign Office was often asked for information on how they were organized in Britain. Few in the House of Commons would have thought it trivial or inappropriate when, in 1943, after the fall of Mussolini, an MP stood up and warned that although we had got Ponsford out cheaply, Bradman was still batting.

Sport has mattered to many Britons, especially men, for a long time now. The myth is a potent one.

In the last sixty-five years, however, sport has become an international phenomenon. Britain is no longer the only sporting nation, nor the leading one. In such circumstances sport cannot be singled out as a unique part of the nation's greatness. Today only the eccentric remain transfixed by the idea that sport uniquely builds character. In fact, more people would probably share the conclusions of two American psychology popularizers who presented a report on research they had done on the personality of athletes under the heading 'Sport. If you want to build character, try something else'.[1] But sport continues to exercise a considerable hold on the imagination of people in almost all contemporary cultures. How it does so is not difficult to explain.

Sport at all levels involves the display and use of physical skill, speed, strength and stamina. Teamwork provides an additional attraction in some sports. Many of the onlookers will have played themselves at sometime in their lives and this will often enhance their appreciation of the supreme physical qualities necessary for playing sport at élite levels. But even in the park the middle-aged can obtain vicarious pleasure from the play of the young.

All sport contains 'a powerful visual aesthetic — bright colours, fast movement, balance, the snaking and coagulating movement of muscles'. And this is accompanied by a spontaneous or live dramatic experience, an experience which is characterized both by the familiar and the unexpected. Those spectators who regularly attend football matches know what is going to take place, but the exact outcome and how it will be brought about remain as much a mystery to themselves as to the players on the field. No two games are ever quite the same — each one contains both the predictable and the unpredictable, resulting in an 'expectation of something that delights'.[2] Chance is ever waiting to intervene.

Again, for players and perhaps even more for spectators, sport erases the consciousness of everyday reality. This does not mean that sport is a separate world neither influencing the society of which it is a part nor being touched by it. But it *is* a world where an escape can, temporarily, be made from life. This has long been recognized from Hazlitt to J. B. Priestley, even to contemporary sociologist Stuart Hall. Hazlitt caught the essence when recommending a motto which might be placed above the Fives Court door: 'Who enters here, forgets himself, his country and his friends'.[3]

The importance of anticipation and recollection is also a crucial part of the value and enjoyment of sport. Bernard Darwin, author and leading golfing journalist of the 1920s and 1930s, thought that there was a substantial number of people of his acquaintance who could take a decent degree in cricket. Not all sports lend themselves to intellectual or statistical study in quite the same way, but the point is well taken. Reading about sport, both events which you may have seen and those many more which you have not, is a vital part of the attraction. And talking about it, either to anticipate future excitements or to recall past memories, is both important in itself and as an ingredient of sociability. 'We always got there early so that we could sit where we wanted to and so as not to risk missing the first notes of the overture, as well as for the pleasure that comes from savouring in anticipation a delightful experience that you know you are about to enjoy.' When Hector Berlioz wrote these words in 1870 he was referring to the opera. They apply just as appositely to sport.[4]

Finally, sport often contributes to an enhancement of the individual's sense of identity with or belonging to a group or collectivity. It can be a district, village, town, city or county. It can be class, colour or country. It can sometimes cut across some, all or most of these. The sporting occasion often simultaneously promotes these emotions and feelings. The excitement so stimulated might be vulgar but it is an elevating experience for all that.

There are today several threats to sport's ability to continue to provide these satisfactions. Violence both on and off the field and discrimination by class, gender or race have already been identified as serious matters for contemporary sport. Drug abuse has also been shown to be present in some sports such as athletics, cycling and weightlifting. Most of these issues are closely bound up with the two major problems which we have already noticed as facing sports in the Britain of the 1980s – namely the cult of winning and the march of commercialization. Partisanship and sport have a long and not always honourable association leading sometimes to chauvinism and savagery, but their cohabitation seems inescapable. People want their own man, their own woman, or their own team to win. There does not seem anything inevitably wrong with this but in modern professional sport – and therefore by imitation and emulation down the grades – being on the winning side appears to have become a dangerous obsession. The absurdity of the victory cult has been most impressively pointed out by Philip Roth in *The Great American Novel*:

'I am talking about *winning*, Roland, *winning* – what made this country what it is today. Who in his right mind can be against that?'
Who, indeed. Winning! oh, you really can't say enough good things about it. There is nothing quite like it. Win hands down, win going away, win by a landslide, win by accident, win by a nose, win without deserving to win – you just can't beat it, however you slice it. Winning is the tops. Winning is the name of the game. Winning is what it's all about. Winning is the be-all and the end-all, and don't let anybody tell you otherwise. All the world loves a winner. Show me a good loser, said Leo Durocher, and I'll show you a loser. Name one thing that losing has to recommend it. You can't. Losing is tedious. Losing is exhausting. Losing is uninteresting. Losing is depressing. Losing is boring. Losing is debilitating. Losing is compromising. Losing is shameful. Losing is humiliating. Losing is infuriating. Losing is disappointing. Losing is incomprehensible. Losing makes for headaches, muscle tension, skin eruptions, ulcers, indigestion, and for mental disorders of every kind. Losing is bad for confidence, pride, business, peace of mind, family harmony, love, sexual potency, concentration, and much much more. Losing is bad for people of all ages, races and religions; it is as bad for

infants as for the elderly, for women as for men. Losing makes people cry, howl, scream, hide, lie, smolder, envy, hate, and quit. Losing is probably the single biggest cause of suicide in the world, and of murder. Losing makes the benign malicious, the generous stingy, the brave fearful, the healthy ill, and the kindly bitter. Losing is universally despised, as well it should be. The sooner we get rid of losing, the happier everyone will be.
'But winning. To win! It was everything Roland remembered.'[5]

A popular consensus among professional sports people and the journalists who record their doings both on and off the field of play is that winning is 'what it's all about'. A more accurate account of what it is all about would also have to address the consequent desire of the professional coaches and players not to lose. To avoid defeat is often a high priority for professional sportsmen and women. Their motto may be summed up as: 'do not give anything away, aim to reach a position from which you cannot lose, then think about winning'. Safety plays in snooker, slow play in snooker and golf, slow over rates and defensive batting in cricket, and the accent on defence in both soccer and rugby are all signs of the fear of defeat. Yet in all these sports someone must lose and lose regularly. In fact without losers there can be no winners. Winners need losers, otherwise they would not be winners. Sport is by definition competitive. But it is important to get the right assessment of winning and losing. Losing has often been likened to death but it is only a little death and it is one of sport's enduring attractions that there is almost always a second chance.

The second major threat to sport lies in its openness to exploitation for commercial ends. We have already noted the growth of sponsorship of sport by commercial companies but sport has become big business in other respects. One 1979 estimate put the total spending on sports goods and equipment at £704 million. Of this sum £202 million was spent on equipment, £272 million on clothing and £130 million on boating. By 1982 the estimated total spent had risen to £822 million.[6]

Spending on sports clothing rose from 19 per cent to 25 per cent of the total sports goods market in the 1970s. The connection between many football clubs and clothing firms has not been very edifying. Clubs have agreed to change their shirts regularly for financial consideration which in turn boosted demand for the new colours among juvenile supporters. Replica shirts, socks and shorts for many first and second division football clubs can cost over £20. But it is the more overt business stance of British sport which is the main threat. Business and sport have never been entirely unconnected in Britain. Boxing promoters, for example, were always eager to make money for themselves and a few did particularly well in the years after the setting up of the British Boxing Board of Control in 1929. But, in the main, once British sport had developed its modern administrative structure – which had been achieved for major sports like athletics, cricket, football, racing and rugby by 1900 – the money-making side of it was kept under control. Not without some difficulty, a little hypocrisy and turning of blind eyes it is true, but in general the entrepreneur was not attracted to sport for the profit which could be made out of it. Football provides a good example of a professional sport in which all the leading clubs were registered as limited liability companies and run by a board of directors responsible to a body of shareholders in the most conventional commercial way. But, as we noticed earlier, dividends were long limited to 5 per cent and directors could not be paid. If profits were made, they were ploughed back. Moreover, it became commonplace for directors to run their football clubs with a negligence of prudent practice which they would never have dreamt of employing in their own firms. Sport was not a legitimate avenue for money-making.

The interesting comparison is with major sports in the United States of America where there was a struggle between those who saw sport as something separate from business and those who saw no reason not to make profit from sport as they would from any other potentially lucrative activity. The American profit maximizers had probably won that battle well before 1914. Even college football was certainly big business by the 1920s, with large crowds drawn to the matches and large revenues ploughed into new stadiums, athletic scholarships and subsidies for more conventional academic activities.

In Britain this did not happen. But in the last fifteen years the balance has apparently shifted, bringing with it four major dangers so far as top-level sport is concerned. First, as we emphasized earlier, commercial sponsors and investing businessmen want to be associated with success. This seems likely to intensify that cult of the winner which we have already identified as one of the major problems of contemporary sport.

Second, sport is over exposed, not only on television but on the fields, courts, tracks, tables and rings of Britain and indeed the wider world. The growth in numbers of tennis tournaments, rugby tours, athletic meetings, cricket test series and football matches is in part due to the need to satisfy existing sponsors or to offer opportunities for more. This market saturation both spoils the public appetite and drains the physical and mental resources of the leading players with whose names and teams every sponsor wishes to be associated. It may lead to a loss of seriousness and spontaneity which in turn will increase the choosiness of the paying public.

Third, in professional team games such as football and rugby league, the new commercialism has created an even greater imbalance between the clubs. The abolition of the maximum wage and the introduction of freedom of contract for the players has increasingly concentrated the best talent in a small number of leading clubs. In soccer, first division clubs have now moved to corner for themselves the lion's share of sponsorship and television money and to retain the bulk of the proceeds from the gate of home matches. The co-operative sharing which has characterized the Football League throughout most of the first century of its existence has disappeared, to be replaced by a more commercially competitive ethos. It is clear that clubs at the top expect this removal of protection for the less well off to allow market forces to push the weakest towards the wall.

Finally the new commercialism may destabilize some sports. The historical and organic way in which most British sports clubs have grown up, closely identified with particular places, will increasingly become irrelevant. Once again it is the most popular spectator sport of football which appears to have travelled the farthest down this road. In the United States, club franchises have been sold and clubs moved in all the major sports of basketball, baseball, football and ice hockey. If a club cannot at least break even in one place then it may be removed to another. In Britain, so far, tradition, invented or not, and the dead weight of the past has resisted similar moves, such as the attempt to merge Oxford United and Reading or move Luton to Milton Keynes, but Bristol Rovers has moved to Bath. Clubs with temptingly valuable urban sites have proved vulnerable to attempts at takeover and asset-stripping. At moments like these the very limited democracy of professional sporting clubs and associations will inhibit action by the average enthusiast. Only the major shareholders of professional football clubs can have much say in the way they are run. Only members of county cricket clubs can hope to influence policy. Of course the average man on the terraces can vote with his feet but with his club under threat of the bailiffs that is a dubious privilege.

Christopher Lasch, writing about American sport in 1977, tried to sum up the problems facing contemporary sport. He said that the degradation of sport was not that it should be taken too seriously but that it should be subjugated to some ulterior purpose be it profits, patriotism, moral training, even health. Sport can hardly avoid some contact with the wider world but Lasch is surely right that if sport is to retain any integrity all those involved in it will need to be extremely wary of the entrepreneur, the chauvinist, the moralist and even the physician, backed up as he may well be by the sports goods industry and a state which sees sport in instrumental terms. If it does not it will fail to 'awaken certain ideas and sentiments to attach the present to the past and the individual to the collectivity' (Emile Durkheim).

# Notes

*1. Introduction: Sport and contemporary society*

1 The Football League, *Report of the Committee of Enquiry into Structure and Finance*, 43pp.

2 They gave up their three-year sponsorship early in 1986 and were replaced in October 1986 by the *Today* newspaper. It lasted less than a year and Barclays Bank took over in 1987.

3 Quoted by Sheila Fletcher, 'The Making and Breaking of a Female Tradition', p.32.

4 This fascinating footnote to both the social history of sport and women is currently being researched by two Gateshead scholars. *Newcastle Evening Chronicle*, March, 1986.

5 As W. J. Baker points out, she would have raised even more eyebrows if her body had been made for display and not action! Baker, *Sports in the Western World*, p.227.

6 The official historian of the AAA cannot enlighten us. Lovesey, *The Official Centenary History of the Amateur Athletic Association*, p.66.

7 The Boston Red Sox did not sign their first black player until 1959.

8 Pascal and Rapping, *Racial Discrimination in Organised Basketball*, p.36.

9 *New Socialist*, July/August 1986, p.24.

10 In Dunning *et al.* 'Football Hooliganism in Britain before the First World War', pp.215–40.

11 On Rangers and Celtic see Murray, *The Old Firm, Sectarianism, Sport and Society in Scotland*.

12 Report of the Working Party on Crowd Behaviour at Football Matches.

13 Cohen, *Folk Devils and Moral Panics*.

## 2. Historical development

1 Roger Eckersley, *The BBC and All That*, p.77.

2 BBC Presentation of Sports, R/30 OB Sports File 2 1947–49 located in the BBC Written Archives Centre at Caversham.

3 *The Guardian*, 13 June, 1985.

## 3. Theory and opinion

1 Rigauer, *Sport and Work*, p.43.

2 Bale, *Sport and Place*, p.100.

3 *Ibid*, p.129.

4 Physical Education Association, *Britain in the World of Sport*, p.45.

5 McIntosh and Charlton, *The Impact of Sport for All Policy*.

6 This is out of an estimated 22 million amateurs and part-timers round the world. *Times*, 14 Sept. 1980.

7 McIntosh and Charlton, p.118.

8 Shaw, *Sport and Leisure Participation and Life Styles in Different Residential Neighbourhoods*, p.45. Bale, *Sport and Place*, p.48.

9 Bale, *Sport and Place*, p.46.

10 Powell, *The Valley of Bones*, p.184.

11 *Alumnus Football*, n.d.

### 4. Comparisons

1 This subject is excellently treated by Grazia, in *The Culture of Consent*, esp. pp.170–5.
2 Told by J. Hoberman, *Sport and Political Ideology*, p.191.
3 Physical Education in Germany, Board of Education Pamphlet, 109 (1937) p.78.
4 Bale, *Sport and Place*, pp.122–4.
5 Much of what follows is based on Childs, 'The German Democratic Republic', pp.67–101; Jurgen Tampke 'Politics Only?' pp.86–98; Hoberman, *Sport and Political Ideology*, pp.202–18.
6 See, for example, Arnot and Gaines, *Sport Selection* (1984) Introd.
7 Hoberman, *Sport and Political Ideology*, p.210.

### 5. Conclusions

1 Bruce C. Ogilvie and Thomas A. Tutko, *Psychology Today*, October 1971, p.61–3.
2 The phrase is David Martin's in a letter to the author 1986.
3 William Hazlitt, *Selected Writings*, p.134.
4 David Cairns (ed.). *The Memoirs of Hector Berlioz*, p.92.
5 Philip Roth, *The Great American Novel*, pp.287–8.
6 See Butson, *The Financing of Sport in the United Kingdom*.

# Bibliography

Allison, L. (ed.), *The Politics of Sport*, Manchester, 1986.

Anthony, D., *A Strategy for British Sport*, London, 1980.

Archer, H. and Bouillon, A., *The South African Game, Sport and Racism*, London, 1982.

Arnot, R. B. and Gaines, C. L., *Sport Selection*, London, 1984.

Baker, W. J., *Sports in the Western World*, New Jersey, 1982.

Bale, J. R., *Sport and Place: A Geography of Sport in England and Wales*, London, 1982.

Birley, D., *The Willow Wand*, London, 1979.

Bowen, R., *Cricket: A History of its Growth and Development Throughout the World*, London, 1970.

Briggs, A., *The History of Broadcasting in the United Kingdom* Vols I, II, IV, Oxford, 1961, 1965, 1979.

Brookes, C., *English Cricket. The game and its players through the ages*, London, 1978.

Butson, P., *The Financing of Sport in the United Kingdom*, Information Series No. 8, Sports Council, 1983.

Cairns, D., (ed.). *The Memoirs of Hector Berlioz*, London, 1981.

Cashman, R. and McKernan, M. (eds.), *Sport in History*, St Lucia, Queensland, 1979.

Cashman, R. and McKernan, M. (eds.), *Sport: Money, Morality and the Media*, Sydney, 1981.

[121]

SPORT IN BRITAIN

Cashmore, E., *Black Sportsmen*, London, 1982.

Central Council for Physical Recreation, *Report of the Committee of Inquiry into Sports Sponsorship*, The Howell Report, London, 1983.

Childs, D., 'The German Democratic Republic'. In J. Riordan (ed.), *Sport under Communism*, London, 1978.

Cohen, S., *Folk Devils and Moral Panics*, London, 1972.

Coldham, J. B., *Lord Harris*, London, 1983.

*Drug Abuse in Sport* London, 1986.

Dunning, E. and Sheard, K., *Barbarians, Gentlemen and Players*, London, 1979.

Dunning, E., Murphy, P., Williams, J. and Maguire, J., 'Football hooliganism in Britain before the First World War', *International Review of Sport Sociology*, 9, 1984, 215–40.

Eckersley, R., *The BBC and All That*, London, 1977.

Fletcher, S., 'The making and breaking of a female tradition: women's physical education in England 1880–1980' *British Journal of Sports History*, 2, May, 1985.

Football League, The, *Report of the Committee of Enquiry into Structure and Finance*, The Chester Report, Lytham St Annes, 1983.

Gordon, Sir H., *Background of Cricket*, London 1939.

Grazia, V. de. *The Culture of Consent: Mass Organization of Leisure in Fascist Italy*, Cambridge, 1981.

Guttmann, A., *From Ritual to Record. The Nature of Modern Sports*, New York, 1978.

Hargreaves, Jennifer (ed.), *Sport, culture and ideology*, London, 1982.

Hargreaves, John, *Sport, Power and Culture*, Oxford, 1986.

Hazlitt, W., *Selected Writings*, London, 1970.

Hoberman, J. M., *Sport and Political Ideology*, London, 1984.

Holt, R., *Sport and Society in Modern France*, London, 1981.

Inglis, S., *Soccer in the Dock. A History of British Football Scandals 1900–1965*, London, 1985.

Jones, S. G., 'Sport, politics and the Labour Movement: the British Workers' Sports Federation, 1923–1935', *British Journal of Sports History*, 2, September, 1985.

[122]

Kircher, R., *Fair Play: The Games of Merrie England*, London, 1928.

Lovesey, P., *The Official Centenary History of the Amateur Athletics Association*, London, 1980.

Mandell, R. D., *The Nazi Olympics*, London, 1972.

Mangan, J. A., *Athletics in the Victorian and Edwardian Public School*, Cambridge, 1981.

Mason, T., *Association Football and English Society 1863–1915*, Brighton, 1980.

McIntosh, P., *Sport in Society*, London, 1963.

McIntosh, P. and Charlton, V., *The Impact of Sport for All Policy 1966–1984 And a Way Forward*, London 1985.

Mews, S., 'Puritanicalism, sport and race: a symbolic crusade of 1911'. In G. J. Cuming and D. Baker (eds.), Popular Beliefs and Practice, *Studies in Church History* 9, 1972, 303–31.

Michener, J. A., *Michener on Sport*, London, 1976.

Midwinter, E., *Fair Game, Myth and Reality in Sport*, London, 1986.

Molyneux, D. D., *Central Government Aid to Sport and Physical Recreation in Countries of Western Europe*, Birmingham, 1962, 51pp.

Murray, W., *The Old Firm. Sectarianism, Sport and Society in Scotland*, Edinburgh, 1984.

Paffenbarger, R. S., Jr., 'Exercise as Protection Against Heart Attack', *New England Journal of Medicine*, 380, 18, 1026–7.

Pankin, R. M. (ed.), *Social Approaches to Sport* New York 1982.

Pascal, A. H. and Rapping, L. A., *Racial Discrimination in Organized Basketball*, Santa Monica, 1976.

Physical Education Association, *Britain in the World of Sport*, London, 1956.

Powell, A., *The Valley of Bones*, London, 1983.

Rigauer, B., *Sport and Work*, translated by A. Guttmann, New York, 1981.

Riordan, J., *Sport in Soviet Society*, Cambridge, 1977.

Roth, P., *The Great American Novel*, London, 1986.

Shaw, M., *Sport and Leisure Participation and Life Styles in Different Residential Neighbourhoods*, Sports Council, 1984.

Smith, D. and Williams, G., *Fields of Praise. The Official History of the Welsh Rugby Union*, Cardiff, 1980.

Sports Council, The, *Sport in the Community: The Next Ten Years*, London, 1982.

Tampke, J., 'Politics only?: Sport in the German Democratic Republic'. In R. Cashman and M. McKernan (eds.), *Sport in History*, St Lucia, Queensland, 1979.

Taylor, I., 'On the sports violence question: soccer hooliganism revisited'. In Jennifer Hargreaves (ed.), *Sport, Culture and Ideology*, London, 1982.

Tomlinson, A. and Whannel, G., (eds.), *Five Ring Circus: Money, Power and Politics at the Olympic Games*, London, 1984.

Trelford, D., *Snookered*, London, 1986.

Vamplew, W., *The Turf. A Social and Economic History of Horse Racing*, London, 1976.

Vamplew, W., 'The economics of a sports industry: Scottish gate-money football, 1890–1914', *Economic History Review*, 35, 1982.

Veblen, T., *The Theory of the Leisure Class. An Economic Study of Institutions*, New York, 1919, ed.

Wagg, S., *The Football World. A Contemporary Social History*, Brighton, 1984.

Whannel, G., *Blowing the Whistle. The Politics of Sport*, London, 1983.

Williams, J. *et al. Hooligans Abroad: The Behaviour and Control of English Fans in Continental Europe*, London, 1984.

# Index

Advertising, 3, 4, 6, 46, 83, 90
Alcock, Charles, 38, 48
Amateurism, 36–46, 53, 73, 88, 89, 103
Annan Report, 56–7
Aston Villa, 5, 27
Amateur Athletic Association, AAA, 9, 19, 21, 37–8, 41, 44
Archery, 9
Athletics, 3, 6, 7, 10, 12, 14, 16, 19, 21, 41, 45, 48–9, 52, 55, 71, 78, 89, 91, 95, 102, 104, 105, 107, 112, 115, 116
*Athletic News*, 48
Amateur Rowing Association, A.R.A., 12
Arlott, John, 59
Australia, 13, 37, 75, 87, 94, 95

Badminton, 79, 83, 84
Bannister, Roger, 103
Baseball, 14, 15, 17, 58, 117, 119
Basketball, 14, 15, 18, 117
Beckett, J., 14
*Bell's Life*, 37, 46–7
Bentley, J.J., 48
Billiards, 3, 40
Birmingham F.A., 23, 27–8
Bolton Wanderers, 29

Bowls, 80, 83, 98
Boxing, 10, 14, 17, 22, 41, 55, 57, 83, 94, 104, 107, 115
Botham, Ian, 21, 88
Brake Clubs, 29
British Amateur Athletic Board, 45
British Boxing Board of Control, 14, 115
BBC (Radio & TV), 52, 53, 56, 57, 58, 78, 84
Brundage, Avery, 11
Butlin, Billy, 78
Budd, Zola, 7
Buses 31, 33

Cardiff City, 31
Celtic, Glasgow, 29
Chelsea, 31, 32
Chester Report, 2
Central Council of Physical Recreation, CCPR, 4, 46, 81, 82, 84–5, 86–8, 92, 102, 112
Class, 7, 8, 12, 18, 22, 28, 30, 31, 32, 33, 34, 36, 39, 40–1, 42, 44, 45, 47, 48, 49, 50, 54, 59, 62, 63, 69, 70–1, 73, 76–7, 78–9, 82, 84–5, 86–8, 92, 102, 112
Coaches, 16, 17, 19, 105, 114
Cornhill Insurance, 5

Commonwealth Games, 14, 57
Coventry City, 15, 34–5
*Cricket*, 48
Cricket, 1, 3, 4, 5, 6, 8, 9, 11, 13, 17,
  21, 23, 24, 36, 38, 39, 42, 43, 44,
  48, 49, 50, 51, 53, 55, 60, 64, 75,
  78, 79, 80, 87, 88, 89, 91, 92, 94,
  95, 103, 110, 112, 114, 115, 116,
  117
Compton, Denis, 42
Comprehensive schools, 91, 92
Croft & Co., 5
Cotton, Henry, 51
Cycling, 19, 20, 21, 112

*Daily Herald*, 49
*Daily Mail*, 49
Darts, 21, 83, 90
Davis, Joe, 51
Deviancy amplification, 33
Diving, 9
Donoghue, Steve, 51
Dopolavoro, 98
Drill, 8
Drink, 6, 29, 31
Drugs, 1, 18–22, 93, 108, 112
Duleepsinhji, K.S., 13

Edrich, W.J., 42
Europe, 2, 19, 21, 66, 76, 94
Everton, 17

Fair play, 44, 53, 86, 88, 95, 96
Fascism, 71
Fédération International de
  Football Association, F.I.F.A., 42,
  98
*Field*, The, 48
Finance, 1, 2, 3, 4, 5, 6, 58, 59,
  64–5, 89–90, 91–2, 101, 102–3,
  106, 108–9, 114, 117
Finland, 80, 104
Fishing, 55, 78, 83, 107
Football coupons, 61, 65
Football pools, 61, 64, 65–6, 67, 68
Football, American, 14, 15, 18, 21,
  70, 85–6, 93, 115–16, 117
Football, 1, 2, 3, 4, 8, 10, 11, 12, 13,
  15–16, 17, 21, 22, 23, 24–9, 30,
  31, 32, 33, 34, 35, 38, 40, 41, 42,
  48, 49, 55, 57, 58, 59, 61, 65, 66,
  67, 71, 78, 80, 83, 84–5, 88–9,

91, 94, 96, 98, 99, 100, 102, 103,
  105, 107, 109, 110, 111, 114,
  115, 116, 117, 119
Football Association, F.A., 3, 11,
  32, 34, 35, 38, 42, 65, 66, 67, 84,
  98, 100
Football League, 2, 3, 16, 28, 29,
  34, 39, 40, 41, 48, 52, 58, 65–6,
  67, 115, 116
*Football Field & Sports Telegram*, 50
FA Cup, 3, 26, 29, 38, 52, 53, 54,
  76, 102
Football hooliganism, 25, 30, 31,
  32, 33, 34, 35
Foreign Office, 96–7, 99–100, 102,
  103, 110
Francis, Roy, 13

Gambling, 39, 40, 47, 48, 49, 53,
  59–68
German Democratic Republic,
  GDR, 10, 12, 94, 104–8
Gillette, 4
Glasgow, 29
Golf, 3, 16, 21, 38, 51, 52, 53, 56,
  78, 79, 83, 90, 107, 112, 114
Gordon, Sir Home, 13
Gould, Arthur, 43
Grace, W.G., 43, 44, 50–1, 88
*Gregory's Girl*, 11
Greyhounds, 19, 64
Grounds, 2, 4, 28, 29–30, 31, 32,
  34–5, 116, 117
*Guardian*, The, 59
Gymnastics, 11, 20, 55, 71, 97, 98,
  104, 105, 107

Hammer, 10
Harris, Lord, 13
Health, 6, 12, 22, 70, 73, 76, 77,
  83–5, 87, 90, 91, 98, 100, 101,
  117
Hendricks, T., 13
Hill, Jimmy, 57
Hobbs, Sir Jack, 51
Hobson, J.A., 62, 70
Hockey Association, H.A., 9
Hockey, 7, 8, 9, 80, 107
Horse racing, 1, 3, 19, 38, 39, 47,
  48, 49, 51, 52, 53, 59, 60, 62, 64,
  67, 68, 89, 90, 115
Horse trials, 5

Honours, 51, 55, 89
Howell, Denis, 81
Hungary, 58
Hutton, Sir Len, 51

Identity cards, 31
Independent Television, ITV, 56, 57, 78
International Amateur Athletic Federation, IAAF, 19, 45
Italy, 29, 31, 57, 66, 71, 94, 95, 96, 97, 98, 110

Jockey Club, 19
Jogging, 12, 85, 90
John Player, 6
Johnson, Jack, 14
Judo, 10

Lancashire County Cricket Club, 53
Lang Report, 30
Latin America, 2, 29, 58, 96
Lawn Tennis Association, LTA, 41
Leeds United, 25, 31, 34
Lewis, Carl, 16
Liverpool F.C., 17, 24–5, 86, 90
London County Council, LCC, 78
Long jump, 16
Luton Town, 34, 117

Magistrates, 29, 30–1, 89
Manchester United, 25, 31, 32
Manliness, 87
Macdonald, J. Ramsey, 63
Marathon, 12, 19, 84, 90, 95, 97
Marxism 69, 72–7
Matthews, Sir Stanley, 51
Marylebone Cricket Club, MCC, 11, 13, 38, 43, 64, 65, 97
Medicine, 20, 106, 108, 117
Membership cards, 34
Meredith, Billy, 51
Minister of Sport, 31, 78, 81, 97, 99
Militarism, 70, 71, 73, 98, 101, 102, 104, 105, 110
Mita Copiers, 5
Motor sport, 1

National Anti-Gambling League, 62–3
National Fitness Council, 101, 102
National Front, 31

Nationalism, 57–8, 70, 73, 87, 96–101, 102, 103, 110, 112, 113, 117
National Playing Fields Association, 78, 80
Nazis, 71, 94, 97, 99–100, 101, 105
*News of the World*, 3, 49
Newspapers and magazines, 3, 12, 33, 36, 46, 47, 48, 49, 50, 51, 52, 61, 62, 78, 90, 93, 96, 101

Olympic Games, 9, 10, 11, 19, 21, 37, 54, 72, 81, 94, 95, 97, 98, 99, 100, 104, 106, 108
Oxford United, 32, 34, 117

Participation, 8, 12, 53, 66–7, 77–85, 91–3, 105–6, 107–8, 111
*Pastime*, 48
Pedestrianism, 3, 36, 39, 59–60
Pentathlon, 10
Perry, Fred, 51
Physical education, 8, 91, 101, 105
Piggott, Lester, 51
Pole vault, 10, 44
Prejudice, 1, 7
Police, 24, 26, 27, 28, 29, 30, 31, 32, 34, 35, 63, 82, 105
Politics, 25, 30, 31, 33, 34, 59, 62, 63, 64, 67, 74–5, 81, 83, 87, 91–2, 94–109
Prize-fighting, 3, 36, 50, 60
Professionalism, 36–46, 60, 64, 73, 86–7, 88, 92, 102, 103, 113, 114
Programmes, 4
Public schools, 8, 22, 38, 40, 43, 46, 78, 87, 88, 92

Racism, 7, 13–18, 31, 33, 112, 119
Radio, 12, 51–4, 57, 58, 61, 90, 102
Railways, 30, 31, 33, 44, 46
Ranjitsinhji, K.S., 13, 51
Recreation grounds, 80
*Referee*, 49
Referees, 17, 23, 24, 25, 27, 28, 47, 52, 81, 102
Richards, Sir Gordon, 51
Rigauer, Bero, 73–7
Rous, Sir Stanley, 66–7, 100
Rowing, 12, 21, 37, 39, 49, 52, 53
Rowntree, B.S., 62

Rugby, 1, 21, 22, 38, 40, 48, 53, 55, 91, 95, 107, 114, 115, 116
Rugby Union, 13, 16, 24, 39, 43, 45, 52, 78, 94
Rugby League, 5, 16, 25, 39, 49, 58, 70, 78, 89, 94, 116
Running, 12, 84, 90
Russia, USSR, 10, 11, 72, 94, 100–1, 103, 104

Sailing, 9, 83, 114
*Saturday Night*, 49
Sayers, Tom, 50
Sexism, 7–12, 31–2, 35, 112, 118
Sex test, 12, 19
School teachers, 18, 35, 80, 91–2, 105
Shot-putting, 11
Showjumping, 55, 83
Sheffield Wednesday, 34
Skating, 9, 11, 55
Smith, Calvin, 16
Snooker, 3, 20, 51, 55, 56, 59, 83, 85, 86, 90, 114
Socialism, 70, 71, 75, 97, 104
Soccer as family entertainment, 35
South Africa, 13, 14, 45
Spain, 29, 66, 96
Spectators, 1, 2, 8, 17, 22, 24, 25, 26, 27, 28, 29, 30, 31, 32, 33, 34, 35, 38, 41, 52, 53, 58, 70, 73, 89, 111, 116
Speedway, 83
Sponsorship, 3, 4, 5, 6, 35, 44, 45, 46, 47, 88, 89, 90, 113, 114, 116, 118
*Sporting Chronicle*, 47
*Sporting Life*, 47
Sports Council, 4, 21, 78, 81, 82, 83, 90–1, 106
*Sportsman*, The, 47
Sportsmanship, 86–8, 90–1, 93
Squash, 55, 78, 79, 84
Street Betting Act, 1906, 59, 63
*Sunday Chronicle*, 49
Swimming, 9, 11, 21, 41, 55, 71, 78, 84, 104, 107, 108
Sunderland FC, 89–90
Sweden, 66, 80, 102

Table tennis, 79, 83

Television, 5, 6, 12, 33, 44, 45, 51, 54–9, 85, 89, 90, 93, 103, 116
Tennis, 4, 8, 9, 11, 16, 21, 41, 51, 53, 55, 58, 78, 79, 80, 83, 105, 107, 116
Test and County Cricket Board, TCCB, 43, 64
Thatcher, Mrs, 31, 93
Thomas, Danny, 15
*The Times*, 49, 62
Tottenham Hotspur, 15, 27, 31
Tour of Britain, 19
Training, 6, 10, 12, 16, 19, 20, 40, 74, 75, 106, 108
Triple jump, 10, 16

Ulbricht, Walter, 104
*Umpire*, The, 49
Umpires, 17
United States of America, USA, 2, 14, 15, 16, 17, 18, 19, 21, 58, 69, 75, 76–7, 86, 93, 95, 99, 103, 104, 115–16, 117, 119
Universities, 3, 8, 36, 37, 38, 43, 49, 52, 78, 105

Veblen, Thorsten, 69–70, 112
Violence, 1, 22–35

Wages, 2, 7, 89–90, 93, 116
Water polo, 10
Weightlifting, 10, 21, 112
Wells, Bombardier Billy, 14
West Ham United, 29, 32
Wimbledon, 9, 41–2, 52, 53, 59, 90
Winning, 5, 6, 43, 44, 55, 56, 72, 74, 85–93, 113–14
Wolfenden Report, 81
Wolverhampton Wanderers, 42
Women, 7–12, 82, 83, 108, 118
Women's Amateur Athletic Association, WAAA, 9, 10, 105
Women's Cricket Association, WCA, 9
Women's World Games, 9
Workers' Sports Movements, 71–2, 100, 104
World Cup, 2, 58, 59, 98
Wrestling, 10

Yorkshire County Cricket Club, 17, 53
*Yorkshire Post*, 25